fat-burner foods

fat-burner foods

Dr Caroline M. Shreeve

hamlyn

First published in Great Britain in 2002 by Hamlyn
a division of Octopus Publishing Group Limited
2–4 Heron Quays
London E14 4JP

ISBN 0 600 60380 6

British Library Cataloguing-in-Publication Data
A catalogue record for this book is available from the
British Library.

Printed and bound in China

10 9 8 7 6 5 4 3 2 1

NOTES

Standard level spoon measures are used in all recipes
1 tablespoon = one 15 ml spoon
1 teaspoon = one 5 ml spoon

Both metric and imperial measurements are given for the
recipes. Use one set of measures only, not a mixture of both.

Ovens should be preheated to the specified temperature.
If using a fan-assisted oven, follow the manufacturer's
instructions for adjusting the time and temperature. Grills
should also be preheated.

Free-range medium eggs should be used unless
otherwise stated.

Fresh herbs should be used unless otherwise stated. If
unavailable, use dried herbs as an alternative, but halve the
quantities.

Pepper should be freshly ground unless otherwise specified.

A few recipes include nuts and nut derivatives. Anyone with a
known nut allergy must avoid these.

Fat-burner Foods is meant to be used as a general reference
and recipe book to aid weight loss. However you are urged to
consult a health-care professional to check whether it is a
suitable weight loss plan for you, before embarking on it.

Contents

Introduction   6

1. Burning Body Fat   10

2. How Fat-burner Foods Work   18

3. The Fat-burner Foods Rapid Fat Loss Plan   28

4. The Fat-burner Foods Basic Stabilizer Plan   42

5. Three Alternative Stabilizer Plans   60

6. Just to Remind You...   108

7. Lighting the Fire Within   116

Appendices: Desirable weight ranges   120

Keeping a record   122

Frequently asked questions   124

Index   126

Introduction

FAT FACTS

Being overweight can be an unbearable burden. How we look strongly influences how most of us feel and, while I'm sure that some people truly believe 'Big is Beautiful', for most of us being fat is the worst aspect of our lives. We long not for model figures but simply to make the best of the bodies we have.

Dieting shifts fat for as long as we maintain the effort. But the joy of reaching our target weight can banish memories of the struggle involved – and sooner or later we drop our guard and return to our old eating patterns. There is nothing surprising about this – we are creatures of habit after all, primed to seek instant gratification. Sadly, though, the backlash of frustration and despair as the weight piles back on can drive us straight into the dreaded yo-yo cycle until, scoffing and starving in turn, we end up weighing more than we did to begin with.

This has given rise to the fallacy that dieting makes you fat. It doesn't. Permanent weight loss eludes us because of the faulty methods we choose for shedding unwanted excess weight. Inevitably, as hunger pangs set in and we start to miss favourite foods, temptation becomes impossible to resist. Add low self-esteem and a secret conviction that we'll never really lose weight, and we set ourselves up to fail.

UNDERSTANDING 'OVERWEIGHT'

To lose weight, we have to use up more energy than we take in from food. For many of us, this means watching what we eat – avoiding comfort snacks and cutting down on sugary and fatty foods – and becoming more physically active. But for some very overweight people, even the strictest diet has little effect. Certainly, most studies have failed to show that obese people eat more than those of normal weight, leading researchers to look at factors other than diet to account for unmovable fat.

Recent findings blame genetic make-up for as much as 80 per cent of the variation in body fat

content that exists between different people. One inherited characteristic recognized among a number of very overweight people affects their bodies' use of calories, particularly when food intake is reduced. Many frustrated dieters will have experienced the sudden cessation of weight loss that occurs when they go for hours without eating and take in fewer than a minimum number of calories over a prolonged period of time (this differs with the individual, but is around 1000–1200 calories daily for women and 1200–1500 for men).

Sensing imminent starvation and in preparation for it, the body hangs on to its fat stores and uses the energy it does derive from food for heat production, digestion and other vital functions as economically as possible. In some overweight people this specific inherited trait makes them far more sensitive than others to a reduced food intake, and their sensitive metabolism shuts down to 'tick-over' speed whenever they try to cut down on what they are eating.

We use about 60 per cent of the energy we obtain from food to keep our vital functions ticking over at rest – this is called the basal metabolic rate (BMR). The average sedentary person uses a further 20 per cent in physical activity, but, by becoming more physically active and undertaking regular exercise, both this and the BMR can be increased in normal weight and overweight people for up to 18 hours after the exercise.

Another well-publicized genetic link, discovered in 1994, was the ob-gene (obesity gene). Its protein leptin, produced in fatty tissue, affects the appetite centre in the brain, interfering with the feeling of fullness that most people experience after eating a certain amount.

DANGERS OF SURPLUS FAT

There may be genetic reasons for your difficulty in losing weight, but that does not mean that you have to join the 'Fat is Fantastic' brigade, bragging how happy you feel in your new extra large outfit. Promoting obesity (which is defined as being 20 per cent or

more over your ideal body weight) is actually dangerous. It is linked with increased risks of heart and blood vessel disorders, including high blood pressure and raised cholesterol, stroke, heart attack and deep vein thrombosis (a blood clot in a calf vein which can pass through the bloodstream to the lungs and is frequently fatal). Gall bladder disease and reflux (heartburn) are much more common in fat people. So, too, are irregular periods in women and infertility. Type II diabetes (which typically affects overweight people as mature adults), snoring and sleep apnoea (a blockage that interferes with breathing during sleep and which carries additional risks for heart attack and stroke) are also associated with being overweight.

Obesity-linked cancers are also common, affecting the large bowel, prostate, uterus, cervix, breasts and ovaries. In addition, orthopaedic problems affect overweight people more severely than lighter people, especially chronic backache and sciatica, and arthritis of the weight-bearing joints, such as the knees, ankles and the joints of the feet.

THE FAT-BURNER FOODS SOLUTION...

Sooner or later, an answer had to be found to the problem of the low energy consumption of obese sufferers. Like hundreds of other doctors and nutritionists, I had been researching the problem for years, and coming up with only a few of the answers. Then, one magical day, a patient called Joe L. walked into my consulting room in Ingham, North Queensland, Australia and handed me a piece of paper.

'I thought you might be interested in this, doc. Me and the wife have been over in Western Australia for a family wedding and we visited cousin Bob, who is awaiting heart surgery. He had been given this diet to enable him to lose weight quickly and safely prior to undergoing a coronary bypass op. That was three months ago – he's lost 24 kilos and the doctors are very pleased with him. He's having the op next week, and he

says he hasn't felt so fit for years.' Intrigued, I studied the seven-day eating plan based on two versions of a nutritious and filling soup, attributed respectively to two different hospitals in Perth, Western Australia. My attempts to discuss the diet with one or other hospital drew a blank. The cardiologists, medical and nursing staff and dieticians to whom I spoke were very cagey about it, and I was left with the impression that Joe's cousin Bob had indeed been given the prescribed diet, but that it was not intended for general use. There are several explanations and I feel that the most likely is that, while most doctors and nutritionists know that it is perfectly possible to get a lot of weight off a patient in a hurry when it is important to do so, for example prior to a life-saving operation, few if any would want publicly to endorse a diet that flies so rampantly in the face of the nutritional establishment.

Whatever the plan's origin, I had a number of very overweight patients on my hands, desperate to lose weight, and I decided to offer it to them to try. Six out of seven agreed readily and I monitored their progress weekly.

Meanwhile, I scrutinized the diet from the view of its fat-burning properties, since I had been researching the use of foods to increase a sluggish (i.e. obese) metabolism. It seemed to fit the bill! My willing guinea pigs were delighted with the results of the diet and claimed never to feel hungry. Further research since has led to the development of the fully fledged Fat-burner Foods Weight Loss Programme, which involves following the Rapid Fat Loss Plan for a fortnight, followed by a weight-balancing fortnight on a Stabilizer Plan, which allows a wider choice of foods and encourages the development of healthier eating habits. The programme works by increasing the rate at which the body burns fat, and was highly successful for 78 per cent of the people I treated.

I'm confident that it can work for you, too.

Dr Caroline M. Shreeve

9

- ▶ **The ingredients of success**

- ▶ **Healthy, nutritionally sound eating plan**

- ▶ **Quick, safe fat loss**

- ▶ **Easily available and filling foods**

- ▶ **Simple, adaptable menus**

- ▶ **Healthy eating for life**

- ▶ **Setting your goal**

- ▶ **Monitoring fat loss**

10

1 Burning Body Fat

the ingredients of success

You've no doubt heard the expressions: 'There are no naughty children, only bad parents' and 'There are no aggressive dogs, only lousy owners'. It is tempting to add: 'There are no failed dieters, only unsuitable diets'. Of course these sayings are grossly unfair in many individual circumstances, but all of them contain an element of truth, which is why I designed the Fat-burner Foods (FBF) Weight Loss Programme.

The Programme's success is based on:

• Healthy, nutritionally sound eating plan

• Quick, safe fat loss

• Good choice and plenty of easily available and filling foods

• Simple, adaptable menus and no calorie counting

• Guidance on healthy eating for life

healthy, nutritionally sound eating plan

Carbohydrates, fats, proteins, fibre, vitamins, minerals and trace elements are all vital for human health. Many of the common, everyday foods that supply these nutrients also speed up the process of burning fat, and the two weeks on the FBF Rapid Fat Loss Plan (see Chapter 3) are based on a selection of these, allowing only a limited choice.

Fresh vegetables form the basis of the diet and can be eaten freely throughout. Brown rice, fruit juice, milk and dairy products, meat and poultry supply carbohydrates, proteins and a little fat over a period of seven days, with the second week being a repetition of the first. This two-week Rapid Fat Loss Plan is nutritionally sustainable over the entire 14-day period.

The two weeks that follow on from the Rapid Fat Loss Plan are your chosen Stabilizer Plan (see Chapters 4–5), which will help to balance your body at its new weight and encourage you to eat from a wider range of foods.

quick, safe fat loss

Unsatisfactory weight loss and the dreaded plateau when excess weight refuses to budge are the most common causes of diet failure. I designed the FBF Weight Loss Programme to overcome these problems, and my patients have lost up to 8.5 kg (19 lb) during their first 14 days on the Rapid Fat Loss Plan. Seventy-eight per cent of them maintained their new weight (or shed a little more) on the Stabilizer Plan, and lost up to a total of 15.5 kg (34 lb) on repeating the cycle (another fortnight on the Rapid Fat Loss Plan and another on the Stabilizer Plan). Importantly, substantial weight loss among slimmers was not confined to the youngest and most active members, but occurred across the whole age spectrum. Success factors included sticking to the plan and reporting considerably fewer temptations to cheat. This is not so difficult when you follow the FBF Rapid Fat Loss Diet for only 14 days at a time.

Most nutritionists recommend losing up to 0.45 kg (1 lb) a week. This would result in a weight loss of 23.6 kg (52 lb) in a year, which is unrealistic for millions of overweight people, who need more immediate proof of success if they are to make the changes necessary for a fat-free future. The vision of a svelte figure in a year's time is a poor substitute for successful weight loss for a wedding, holiday or other occasion only three months away.

Fast weight reduction is often regarded as unsatisfactory – attributed mainly to water loss and quickly regained when normal eating is resumed – and unsafe because of the danger of destroying muscle tissue. If this is the case, why have I designed a programme slashing weight by up to 8.5 kg (19 lb) in the first 14 days, and by similar amounts whenever the FBF Rapid Fat Loss Plan is followed thereafter?

The reasons are that, first, the FBF Weight Loss Programme does in fact *melt* surplus fat. The body naturally sheds some fluid in the early stages of fat reduction, but this is by no means solely responsible for the dramatic weight losses on the Rapid Fat Loss Plan. All my patients drank their eight large glasses of water a day, and none of them suffered from kidney failure or became dehydrated or waterlogged!

Second, the choice and combination of foods on the Rapid Fat Loss Plan encourages the body to burn up its own fat rather than attacking muscular tissue. When you cut down your intake of carbohydrates and fat to the extent that your calorie requirements are not met, the body turns to its own surplus fat stores as a source of additional energy. It becomes, in fact, a fat-burning machine. When the Rapid Fat Loss Plan, consisting largely of plant foods and protein, sets this in motion, a metabolic process named ketosis kicks in. Essentially what happens is that some of the fat removed from your fat stores is incompletely burned, leading to the production of waste products called ketones. These ketones are excreted by the kidneys, and their presence in the urine (evident from a simple dip-stick test) is a sign that your body's fat-burning has gone into fast-forward mode. Mild ketosis also curbs the appetite and promotes a feeling of increased energy and wellbeing.

case study

Polly G., a 36-year-old housewife and mother, was 54.5 kg (120 lb) overweight when she came to see me and hating every minute of it. No diet had worked for her in the past and she despaired of any helping her in future. For Polly, The FBF Weight Loss Programme was a last resort! Unsurprisingly, her blood pressure and blood cholesterol were high and she had shown symptoms of early diabetes in her most recent (third) pregnancy. Her BMI (Body Mass Index, see page 17) was 34. She started on the Rapid Fat Loss Plan, recording her weight daily and checking in weekly for me to monitor her progress.

Polly lost an average of 3.5 kg (8 lb) a week on the Rapid Fat Loss Plan, and 1 kg (2 lb) a week on the Stabilizer Plan. After the first month (a fortnight on each plan), she had lost 9.5 kg (21 lb), and it took her just six months to lose her excess weight. Her cholesterol, blood pressure and glucose tolerance test (for diabetes) were normal, and her BMI had dropped to 24. She was playing badminton again and power walking regularly. She felt and looked 10 years younger.

easily available and filling foods

There is nothing complicated about the foods you will eat while you are busy burning off fat. You will find many of your favourites listed in the menu plans and lists, and may already have some in your storecupboard and refrigerator. Fresh fruit and vegetables, meat, fish and poultry can all be combined in recipes you enjoy normally to boost the body's fat-burning capacity.

You need never feel hungry on the FBF Weight Loss Programme. You are encouraged on the Rapid Fat Loss Plan to eat as many raw and lightly cooked fresh vegetables as you like, while the Stabilizer Plan utilizes a wide range of fat-burning foods, with tempting recipes and menus to help you make full use of them.

simple, adaptable menus

Few of us diet in isolation. There is usually the family to cater for and, even if you live alone, there are packed lunches, meals out, holidays and entertaining to take into account.

You have to be quite single-minded on the Rapid Fat Loss Plan, but you follow it for only 14 days at a time and the Stabilizer Plan gives plenty of menu ideas to suit a variety of situations. No special cooking is necessary. The recipes are easy and involve little weighing or measuring. There's no calorie counting, either. The secret is knowing which foods help to burn up fat, and how and when to eat them.

healthy eating for life

For many of us, overindulgence in the past has helped pile on the weight. We know that we will have to eat differently in the future in order to maintain our new weight.

The Stabilizer Plan helps you do this by introducing a wide range of fat-burning foods in recipes you can continue using to maintain your target weight.

setting your goal...

Setting a specific goal when planning to shed surplus weight greatly improves your chances of success. Vague aims, such as 'I'd like to be healthier', or 'I think I'll lose a few kilos or pounds', tend to produce half-hearted efforts and poor results. Be clear in your mind about what you are going to achieve before starting on the FBF Weight Loss Programme. Write it down and put it where you will see and reread it several times a day. 'I am going to lose 6.25 kg (14 lb)' or 'I am going to go down three dress/shirt sizes' will trigger the positive thinking essential for personal growth.

Affirmations, positive statements about yourself or your intentions, are a deceptively simple aid to achieving a goal. They work by imprinting themselves upon the subconscious mind through regular repetition – saying, reading or, best of all, writing them down over and over again.

You can even record them on a suitable tape and listen to them when you are most open to their suggestive influence, for example when you are drowsy and have just woken up or you are about to fall asleep. Do whatever works best for you.

If you truly mean your affirmations and want them to come true, then they will. They do require a little discipline, but their benefits normally far outweigh the time and effort involved. If you are going to repeat them verbally, look in a mirror, smile and speak as though you mean it. Here are some ideas to get you started.

- **'I love life!'**
- **'I love myself!'**
- **'I'm a powerful, confident person!'**
- **'I'm becoming healthy and fit!'**
- **'My body is burning up fat!'**
- **'I'm becoming slimmer daily!'**

monitoring fat loss

You can monitor fat rather than weight reduction by using plastic skin callipers, which measure the thickness of fat in various body areas. You can also go by your Body Mass Index or BMI (see the box below). Callipers are inexpensive and available from good pharmacies. They should come with a chart indicating healthy and unhealthy fat thicknesses. However, they tend to pinch the skin and you will have to enlist help when applying them to inaccessible body areas, such as the upper back.

The easiest way to check your body fat content is with a custom-designed body fat monitor machine. Since body fat content is an individual issue, you need to key in details of your height, age, sex and whether you are an athlete or not, in order to gain an accurate measurement.

Body Mass Index (BMI)

Obesity is defined as being 20 per cent or more above one's desirable weight range. It refers mainly to excess body fat. It is technically possible to be 'overweight' in this way without a spare tyre or love handle in sight. Since muscle is heavier than fat, body builders and athletes often weigh much more than others of the same sex, height and build. No one, though, would call them obese. Conversely, there are also apparently thin people carrying layers of surplus fat.

Body Mass Index (BMI) is a more accurate indicator of surplus body fat than kilos or pounds, although massively muscled athletes – and others who have inherited an unusually heavy build – would still be the exception to the rule. You can calculate your BMI as follows:

BMI = Weight (in kilograms)
÷ Height (in metres) squared
or
Weight (in pounds) x 700
÷ Height (in inches) squared

For example, the calculation for someone weighing 80 kg (176 lb) and 1.60 m (63 in) tall is:
BMI = $80 \div (1.60 \times 1.60) = 31.2$
or
BMI = $176 \times 700 \div (63 \times 63) = 31.1$

Body weight categories according to Body Mass Index (BMI):

Category	BMI
Underweight	under 19
Normal	20–25
Overweight	26–30
Obese	over 30

- ▶ **Accelerating fat-burning**

- ▶ **Thermogenic effect of protein**

- ▶ **Negative calorie foods**

- ▶ **Carbohydrates and carbohydrate foods**

- ▶ **Glycaemic index**

- ▶ **Dietary fats**

- ▶ **Iodine and chromium**

- ▶ **Hydroxycitric acid**

- ▶ **Fat-burner foods**

2 How Fat-burner Foods Work

accelerating fat-burning

Fat-burner foods and human metabolism are highly complex issues and not yet fully understood even by nutritional scientists, so the account of them here is necessarily highly simplified and incomplete.

Certain foods and eating habits can be used to accelerate fat-burning, either directly by promoting the 'meltdown' of the body's surplus fat stores, or indirectly by fine-tuning our use of energy. Protein, for instance, significantly increases the metabolic rate (the pace at which we use food fuel), creating heat and burning many more calories than carbohydrates or fat. Negative calorie foods are those foods that use up more calories in the process of their assimilation into the body than they supply for its use. Certain sources of carbohydrates (i.e. those with the least effect on our blood sugar levels) help us to burn up the food at our disposal rather than storing it as fat. Particular food combinations, for example

protein and negative calorie foods, can be used to mobilize fatty deposits for conversion into energy, a metabolic process called ketosis (see page 14).

Depending on their nature, the fats in our diet affect – either beneficially or adversely – how we respond to insulin, a hormone produced by the pancreas. Insulin controls both the fat content of our cells and our blood sugar levels. Chromium and iodine, two vital minerals, also influence insulin and other hormones concerned with obesity.

Lastly, certain naturally occurring substances, such as caffeine, capsaicin (found in chillies), chitin from shellfish shells, the Chinese herb *Ma Huang*, even aspirin (originally derived from willow bark) influence the way our bodies' handle fat. Another example is hydroxycitric acid, found in the brindleberry fruit, which hinders the production of fats from carbohydrates and curbs the appetite.

thermogenic effect of protein

While 1 gram of fat provides about 9 calories, 1 gram of carbohydrate provides about

4 calories and 1 gram of protein also provides about 4 calories. These statistics explain why most

slimming diets cut down on fat. However, although fat provides, weight for weight, more than twice the energy of the other two food groups, protein has a built-in factor known as its thermogenic effect or 'specific dynamic action', which burns calories and depletes fat stores.

The very act of eating uses calories, since all food requires energy for its breakdown and digestion, absorption from the stomach and small bowel, chemical changes in the bloodstream, liver and so on, and the storage of its nutrients. But while fat has a thermogenic effect of only 0–3 per cent and carbohydrates of 5–10 per cent, protein has one of 20–30 per cent of its calorific value.

This useful, thermogenic effect of food is reduced to 50–150 calories a day in obese people with a resistance to insulin (see below), so increasing the importance of protein in a fat-loss programme, and of other measures which help to sharpen insulin sensitivity.

negative calorie foods

Negative calorie foods use more calories to break down, digest and assimilate them than they supply. The surplus calories 'burn' fat in the body. For example, a portion of fruit trifle provides a total of 350 calories; 100 calories are utilized in digestion and absorption, leaving 250 calories to be added to your day's total calorie intake. However, a portion of Brussels sprouts provides 50 calories; 75 calories are utilized in digestion and absorption, thus burning 25 calories of body fat. Eating mainly negative calorie foods is said to reduce weight three times faster than fasting and to reduce body weight by an average of 0.5 kg (1 lb) a day. It is difficult to confirm these claims, but the concept of negative energy and fat-burning is at least feasible. Since many of the foods are either high-protein or low-GI carbohydrates (see page 22), they are included in the programme.

To help one's metabolism 'burn fat 24 hours a day', however, oxygen consumption must be increased, in the form of either planned aerobic exercise such as brisk walking, cycling or swimming, or specific breathing exercises (see page 118).

carbohydrates

All carbohydrates raise the level of glucose in the blood, which in turn triggers the release of insulin from the pancreas. The job of insulin is to drive the glucose out of the bloodstream and into the cells of muscles and other tissues throughout the body, where it can be combined with oxygen to produce energy, or its surplus can be stored as fat. Refined foods rich in sugars, such as sweets and chocolate, rapidly raise the blood glucose level. The large amounts of insulin released in response can lead to hypoglycaemia (low blood sugar), and by eating large quantities of these refined, high-sugar foods, we gradually blunt our sensitivity to insulin. We need more and more of it to keep our blood glucose within normal limits and, in time, the level of insulin in the blood becomes permanently raised. This insulin resistance greatly increases the risk of developing diabetes and heart disease.

Complex carbohydrates (fruits, pulses, grains and cereals) have a less dramatic effect on our blood sugar level because the fibre they contain causes their starches and sugars to be released more gradually. Smaller amounts of insulin are released as a result, the blood sugar level rises (and falls) more smoothly, and the risk of hypoglycaemia is removed.

glycaemic index

Nowadays, carbohydrates are classed according to the glycaemic index (GI), which reflects their effects on blood glucose level. Foods with a high GI, for example soft drinks and glucose sweets, cause a rapid, large rise in blood glucose, and those with a low GI, such as jacket potatoes, brown rice and wholewheat pasta, cause only a small, slow rise. Eating low-GI carbohydrates helps us to keep our blood glucose level as even as possible (especially important for diabetics) and also plays an important role in energy

ADVANTAGES OF EATING LOW-GI CARBOHYDRATE FOODS:

✔ Normal sensitivity to insulin
✔ Normal levels of circulating glucose, which helps the body to burn up fat
✔ Use of both glucose and body fat to generate energy
✔ Easier weight maintenance
✔ Lower levels of total and LDL (bad) cholesterol, and higher levels of HDL (healthy) cholesterol concentrations

usage and fat burning. The detrimental effects of a high-carbohydrate diet on blood plasma, glucose, insulin and blood fats occur only when foods of a high GI are consumed. They are abolished if the diet is mainly based on fibre-rich, low-GI foods.

Recent studies have shown that consuming carbohydrate-rich foods with a low GI produces lower levels of circulating glucose: this results in more body fat being burned. A bonus is that eating foods with a low GI brings about lower levels of total and 'bad' cholesterol and higher levels of 'good' cholesterol. These findings also show that a high intake of rapidly absorbed carbohydrates increases the risk of coronary heart disease, independent of conventional risk factors such as smoking, being overweight and high blood pressure. By contrast, certain fruits and vegetables, previously considered less than desirable simple carbohydrates, in fact have a low GI.

LOW-GI CARBOHYDRATE FOODS
Breads: multigrain breads (white and brown), heavy fruit breads
Grains and breakfast cereals: brown rice, wild rice, other whole grains, tabbouleh, pearl barley, wholewheat pasta, oats/porridge, unsweetened muesli, high-fibre wheatbran cereal
Vegetables: sweet potato, okra, mushrooms, legumes (peas, beans), broccoli, artichokes, aubergines
Fruits: apples, pears, oranges, mandarins, grapefruit, bananas
Other: honey, jam, soya milk and its products

INTERMEDIATE-GI CARBOHYDRATE FOODS
Breads: sourdough bread, pitta bread, light rye bread
Grains and breakfast cereals: long grain rice, white pasta, whole grain wheat cereal bisks
Vegetables: potatoes
Fruits: plums, strawberries, red/black/whitecurrants, raisins

HIGH-GI CARBOHYDRATE FOODS
Breads: white bread, wholegrain bread
Grains and breakfast cereals: short grain rice; toasted rice cereal
Vegetables: instant potato, tomatoes, lettuce, red cabbage, peppers, marrow
Fruits: watermelon, dried dates
Other: soft drinks, most confectionery

23

dietary fats

A high total fat intake also lowers insulin sensitivity. Conversely, monounsaturated fats have a beneficial effect. An Italian study conducted by G. Ricardi and reported in the *British Journal of Nutrition* in 2000, gave 162 healthy adults a diet high in either monounsaturated or saturated fat, for three months. Results showed that the former significantly improves insulin sensitivity compared with a diet high in saturated fat (fat derived from animal products). However, this beneficial effect disappears when the total fat intake accounts for more than 38 per cent of the total calories consumed.

However, trying to eliminate fat from the diet completely is unhealthy. It is a vital, life-giving nutrient and, if we don't eat as much fat as we need, our bodies make it. Nor do reduced-fat diets in themselves create weight loss. This point is illustrated in the results from a study in the US. In 1955, Americans were getting 40 per cent of their calories from fat; by 1995 the percentage had fallen to 35; in the same period the percentage of overweight adults increased from 25 per cent to 40 per cent. It seems that many people construe a low-fat diet as licence to eat as much as they want of other foods, regardless of calorie content. At the same time, all developed societies are becoming increasingly sedentary, which is another important factor.

Fat will not create extra fat in your body unless you take in more calories than you use. The healthy approach is to keep your energy intake from fats below 38 per cent, cut down saturated fat and include a significant proportion of olive oil and its products and oily fish, such as sardines, mackerel, salmon and tuna, which contain the essential fatty acids.

Unsaturated fats

Our main source of monounsaturated fat is olive oil, the cold-pressed extra virgin variety being the healthiest. Derived from the first pressings of ripe olives, it is crammed with nutrients undamaged by the industrial heat-processing which alters and destroys them. Omega-3 oils, polyunsaturated fats found in fish, seafood, green leafy vegetables and walnut oil, reduce unhealthy blood fats and help guard against heart attacks. Both oily fish and cold-pressed extra virgin olive oil are used extensively in the FBF Weight Loss Programme.

24

iodine and chromium

Iodine is necessary for the normal function of the thyroid gland, which controls the BMR (basal metabolic rate) (see page 7). Iodine deficiency can result in thyroid underactivity, thereby lowering the BMR and causing an increase in weight. Losing weight when one has low levels of thyroxine – the main hormone produced by the thyroid, and which cannot be manufactured without iodine – is practically impossible without some form of medical treatment.

Whether supplemental iodine does help to speed up a sluggish BMR in the absence of a proven deficiency is a moot point. Kelp (a seaweed) is a rich source of iodine, which explains why it is often included in patent slimming formulas. Besides seaweeds, iodine is present in sea fish, seafood and sea salt.

Chromium is required by the body to help it deal with carbohydrates and dietary fats. Combined with the B vitamin nicotinic acid (niacin) and tryptophan or some other amino acid, it constitutes the glucose tolerance factor (GTF chromium), which decreases insulin resistance and drives circulating glucose into the tissues. Diets high in carbohydrates can lead to chromium deficiency; this, as well as the ageing process, impairs the body's ability to make GTF chromium, so then specific foods and supplements are required.

Chromium supplements have been used to improve blood glucose control in sufferers of both Type I diabetes (where the body lacks its own insulin) and Type II (late-onset) diabetes and have reduced their insulin and other medication requirements in some instances. Chromium also promotes the uptake of amino acids (the breakdown products of protein digestion), thereby helping to increase lean body mass (LBM) and decrease stored body fat.

Foods rich in chromium include brewer's yeast, oysters, beef, wholewheat products, potatoes and liver, all of which appear in recipes in the FBF Weight Loss Programme. However, a daily chromium supplement, chromium picolinate, of 400 micrograms (mcg) is recommended as part of the Rapid Fat Loss Plan to accelerate fat burning.

hydroxycitric acid

The rind of the brindleberry fruit is widely used in Asian cooking, as a flavouring in curries instead of limes or tamarind. According to scientific reports (in the *Journal of Biological Chemistry* in 1971 and the *American Journal of Clinical Nutrition* in 1977), the hydroxycitric acid (HCA) found in the rind can inhibit the production of cholesterol and other blood fats from dietary carbohydrates.

Dietary carbohydrates are broken down into glucose. Some is used for energy and the rest is stored as glycogen in the muscles and liver. Once the glycogen stores become full, an enzyme named ATP-citrase lyase turns any excess glucose molecules into cholesterol and fat. HCA appears to inhibit this last stage, reducing fat production by between 40 and 70 per cent for up to 12 hours after a meal. HCA also curbs the appetite, because excess glucose is no longer being turned into fatty tissue and therefore remains stored as glycogen. Glycogen stores remaining at a high level signal to the brain that energy reserves are full and no more food is required.

HCA is also thought to be the active ingredient in the juice and rind of grapefruit and possibly other citrus fruits, which have similar effects to brindleberry. Grapefruit and citrus fruits are therefore included in a fat-burning diet, while brindleberry is best taken as a dietary supplement (available from healthfood stores).

note

The list of negative calorie foods opposite is incomplete, but covers the main foods you enjoy and are used to eating. Use your judgement about others; for example since cress is included, it is fine to use similar sprouting vegetables, such as alfalfa, fenugreek, radish and mung bean sprouts. All raw or lightly cooked vegetables, fruits and nuts in their natural state, provide negative calories, while dried and canned fruits and roasted salted nuts do not.

OTHERS
Cold-pressed extra virgin olive oil and its products
Iodine-rich foods: e.g. edible seaweed such as kombu and nori; sea salt, fish and shellfish
Chromium-rich foods: e.g. brewer's yeast, beef, oysters, wholewheat products, liver and potatoes
Brindleberry and citrus fruits

Fat-burner foods

Some fat-burning foods belong in more than one class, for example negative calorie foods and low-GI, or negative calorie and protein. For simplicity's sake, the foods are grouped under the main class to which they belong. See page 23 for low-GI foods.

FAT-BURNER PROTEIN FOODS

Lean meat: beef, pork, lamb, veal, venison, rabbit, hare, offal

Poultry: chicken, turkey, pheasant, grouse, guinea fowl

Fish: cod, haddock, plaice, sole, coley, whiting, mackerel, trout, salmon

Shellfish: scallops, shrimp, prawns, lobster, crab, scampi, cockles, mussels, winkles, whelks, abalone

Cheese: mainly low-fat cottage cheese and low-fat fromage frais. Use reduced-fat versions of hard cheeses, such as Cheddar, in moderation

Eggs

Soya products

NEGATIVE CALORIE FOODS

Vegetables: asparagus, aubergine (eggplant), beetroot, broccoli, Brussels sprouts, cabbage, carrots, cauliflower, celeriac, celery, chicory, Chinese cabbage (pak choi, bok choy), cress, dandelion leaves, endive, fennel, globe artichokes, green beans, leeks, lettuce, mangetouts (snow peas), mooli (daikon or Japanese radish), mushrooms, okra (ladies' fingers), onions, radishes, seaweed, spinach, squash, swede, tomatoes, turnips

Fruits: apples, apricots, bananas, blackberries, blackcurrants, blueberries, boysenberries, cherries, clementines, cranberries, damsons, figs, gooseberries, grapefruit, grapes, greengages, guavas, kiwi fruit, kumquat, loquat, lychees, mandarins, mangos, medlars, melons, mulberries, nectarines, oranges, papaya, peaches, pears, persimmons, pineapple, plums, pomegranate, prickly pear, raspberries, redcurrants, satsumas, star fruit, strawberries, whitecurrants

Nuts: almonds, Barcelona nuts, Brazil nuts, chestnuts, coconuts, filberts, hazelnuts, macadamias, peanuts, pine nuts, pistachios, walnuts

▶ Starting the plan

▶ Charting your progress

▶ The principles

▶ Rapid Fat Loss Plan guidelines

▶ The 14-day Rapid Fat Loss Plan

▶ Recipes

3 The Fat-burner Foods Rapid Fat Loss Plan

starting the plan

The diet is an extremely healthy one (as we saw in Chapter 2) and suitable for most people (but see below). However, I always err on the side of caution and, because I have never met you and cannot, therefore, monitor your progress, I advise you simply to check first with your own doctor. This is especially important if you suffer from any ongoing health problems, take regular medications and/or you are a teenager or over 65 years old.

After the initial fortnight on the Rapid Fat Loss Plan, the FBF Stabilizer Plan – of which there are four versions in all (see Chapters 4 and 5) – gives you a chance to acclimatize to your new weight and eat a wider range of foods. It is generally rather less demanding than the FBF Rapid Fat Loss Plan and, although most people could safely repeat the first fortnight without a break, the 28-day programme suits most slimmers best.

health check

Check with your doctor before starting the Fat-burner Foods Weight Loss Programme if you have any health concerns or are being treated for a serious or long-standing medical condition. It is also imperative for you to obtain your doctor's approval if you are under 20 or over 65 years of age. Children, adolescents and elderly people have specific nutritional needs that the Fat-burner Foods Weight Loss Programme does not undertake to meet. Your doctor will be able to tell you whether the programme is right for you.

charting your progress

There are also important psychological benefits to be had from following a programme for a specific time. You can keep tabs on your progress by crossing off the days on a calendar to encourage you to keep going, and filling out the 14-day charts of your weight loss provided on pages 122–123.

The FBF Weight Loss Programme leaves nothing to chance: your need for variety, short-term goals and personal feel-good factor are all taken into account in this plan. This is why it can help you to succeed, whatever difficulties you may have experienced with dieting in the past.

Despite all you have read in the past about weighing yourself only weekly (or actually throwing your scales away), dieters on the FBF Weight Loss Programme should weigh themselves daily. Unexpectedly high losses on some days will sustain you over the day or so when your weight appears to get stuck – you are not failing, it's just your body and metabolism adjusting themselves to the effects of fat-burning foods.

positive indicators

✔ You have generally good health

✔ You are aged between 20 and 65

✔ You eat most common foods

✔ You do not suffer from any food allergies or only from allergies with which you can safely cope

✔ You can organize your meals around the complete Fat-burner Foods Weight Loss Programme

the principles

The FBF Rapid Fat Loss Plan provides all the essential nutrients over a seven-day period (the second week is a repeat of the first), and helps you to burn body fat mainly through the use of negative calorie foods (see page 21). Eat the Fat-burning Soup daily at mealtimes and as a snack whenever you feel peckish. Remember, you need *never* go hungry on the FBF Weight Loss Programme.

You will notice that the main omissions from the FBF Rapid Fat Loss Plan are of fruit and vegetables with a high sugar/starch content, and of fatty or oily meat and fish. Some of these will appear in recipes elsewhere in this book. They are excluded here because the FBF Rapid Fat Loss Plan is based upon the simplest and healthiest foods with a negative calorie content. Lean meats others than those mentioned can be eaten (see negative calorie foods list, page 27); but 'treated' foods containing these meats, such as ham, sausages, canned and preserved meats, should be avoided for the time being.

Use organic ingredients whenever possible – you will have to use your common sense about these. Fresh organic foods are becoming increasingly widely available and less expensive. Organic honey is now widely available – choose clear, set or honeycomb, depending on the recipe. Choose between white and black ground pepper, green, pink or other peppercorns as liked, unless specified by the recipe. Spices, such as chilli powder and cayenne pepper, help to accelerate fat-burning. Salt is not an ingredient in any of these recipes; however, use a potassium (low-sodium) salt substitute if you dislike the taste of unsalted vegetables and other savoury dishes.

Rapid Fat Loss Plan Guidelines

DO

✔ Follow the eating plan exactly. Substitute only as suggested.

✔ Drink at least 8 large (300 ml/½ pint) glasses of plain, bottled or filtered water daily, plus herbal teas, tea and coffee, if you wish, without milk or sweetener.

✔ Remove all skin and fat from meat and poultry.

✔ Eat your Fat-burning Soup (see page 36) or snack on raw salad vegetables from the negative calorie foods list (see page 27) whenever you feel hungry.

✔ Use only the recommended dressings for salads and other dishes.

✔ Weigh yourself naked first thing every morning, after going to the toilet. Record your weight on a chart (see pages 122–123).

DON'T

✖ Drink alcohol, soft drinks, fruit juices or beverages with sugar or milk, except as indicated in the recipes.

✖ Use artificial sweeteners if you can avoid them – your taste buds will soon get used to the different taste.

✖ Buy sad-looking fruit or vegetables, or any foods past their sell-by date. The message is fresh, fresh, fresh!

✖ Be tempted by offers of snacks or other foods – this programme is for *your* benefit.

✖ Gulp food. Instead, savour its smell, taste and texture, chewing slowly and thoroughly.

The 14-Day Rapid Fat Loss Plan

	DAY 1 & DAY 8	DAY 2 & DAY 9	DAY 3 & DAY 10
BREAKFAST	• Mango Smoothie (see page 38) or Melon and Grape Salad (see page 38).	• Chilled Fat-burning Soup (see page 36). • Platter of lightly cooked vegetables.	• Mango Smoothie (see page 38), Melon and Grape Salad (see page 38) or mixed fruit.
LUNCH	• Fat-burning Soup (see page 36). • Soft fruit: 3–4 plums, greengages or apricots, a bunch of cherries or currants, or a peach or nectarine.	• Fat-burning Soup (see page 36) with chicory leaves to dunk. • Big bunch of steamed asparagus or broccoli, dressed with Farmhouse Dressing (see page 80).	• Fat-burning Soup (see page 36) with apple slices or chicory to dunk. • Soft fruit.
DINNER	• Fat-burning Soup (see page 36) with apple slices to dunk. • Fresh fruit platter – sliced apple, pear, grapes, plum or greengage, pineapple and peach, sliced, conserving as much juice as possible.	• Fat-burning Soup (see page 36). • Spicy Baked Potato (see page 40). • Braised Vegetables with Dill and Mustard (see page 37).	• Fat-burning Soup (see page 36). • Vegetable platter. • Fresh fruit salad.
NOTES	• Snacks: any fresh fruit, except bananas and tropical fruit with a high sugar content. • Drink at least 8 large glasses of water.	• Eat as many raw or cooked vegetables as you like, except peas, pulses, corn, parsnips, yams, sweet potatoes. • Drink at least 8 large glasses of water.	• Eat any fresh fruit as in Day 1 and any raw or cooked vegetables as in Day 2. • Drink at least 8 large glasses of water.

DAY 4 & DAY 11	DAY 5 & DAY 12	DAY 6 & DAY 13	DAY 7 & DAY 14
• Milkshake made with skimmed milk and banana.	• 125 g (4 oz) lean steak, dry-fried, with sliced tomatoes and a spoon of tomato salsa.	• Dry-fried lean steak and mushrooms.	• Carrot and Celery Juice (see page 59).
• Fat-burning Soup (see page 36). • 2 bananas.	• Fat-burning Soup (see page 36). • Dry-fried lean steak. • Tomato and chicory or cress salad with Farmhouse Dressing (see page 80).	• Fat-burning Soup (see page 36). • Rainbow Salad (see page 80).	• Fat-burning Soup (see page 36). • Warm Rice Salad with Lemon, Garlic and Herbs (see page 41).
• Fat-burning Soup (see page 36). • 2 chopped bananas sprinkled with freshly grated nutmeg.	• Fat-burning Soup (see page 36). • Lean steak and tomatoes as for breakfast or lunch. Or, stir-fry tomatoes without oil, with a handful of spinach or watercress added at the end of cooking.	• Fat-burning Soup (see page 36). • Dry-fried lean steak. • Primavera Stir-Fry (see page 39).	• Fat-burning Soup (see page 36). • Oriental Risotto (see page 41).
• Have up to 8 bananas and 1.2 litres (2 pints) skimmed milk, plus the 8 glasses of water. • Expect a weight loss of 1.75–3 kg (4–7 lb) by day 4.	• Try to eat 300–625 g (10–20 oz) of lean steak and 500 g (1 lb) canned tomatoes or 6–7 fresh tomatoes. • Drink at least 8 large glasses of water.	• You can choose any vegetables you like from the negative calorie foods list (see page 27). • Drink at least 8 large glasses of water.	• Make as much fresh juice as you like from produce on the negative calorie foods list (see page 27). • Drink at least 8 large glasses of water.

Fat-burning Soup

You can vary the total weight of the fresh vegetables – use 250–500 g (8 oz–1 lb) at a time and make up a fresh supply of the soup at least every two days – keep it in the refrigerator. You can substitute one or more of the vegetables with an equal weight of any you prefer on the negative calorie foods list (see page 27). Wash all the vegetables, but do not peel them. The more finely you slice and chop them, the more quickly and evenly they will cook.

Makes 900 ml–1.2 litres (1½–2 pints)

2 bunches of spring onions or 1 large
   onion/leek, finely chopped
1 medium or ½ large cauliflower, divided into
   florets (include the green leaves) or
   2 medium or 1 large head of broccoli
125 g (4 oz) spinach or ½ small
   cabbage, chopped
1 large red, green or yellow pepper, cored,
   deseeded and chopped
6–8 celery sticks, chopped
2–3 large carrots, thinly sliced
1–2 teaspoons each crushed cumin and
   coriander seeds (optional)
1 quantity Home-made Chicken or Vegetable
   Stock (see page 37)
4–5 large ripe tomatoes, quartered or 400 g
   (13 oz) can tomatoes
juice of ½ large lemon or 1 lime
small handful of coriander or flat leaf parsley,
   roughly chopped
2 garlic cloves, finely chopped or
   crushed (optional)
¼–½ teaspoon cayenne pepper (optional)

1 Place all the vegetables except the tomatoes in a large saucepan with the crushed spices, if using. Add the stock and extra water, if necessary, to cover. Heat gently until nearly boiling, then add the tomatoes and the lemon or lime juice.

2 Add the herbs and garlic, if using. Season to taste with cayenne pepper, if liked.

3 Simmer the soup for 20–30 minutes, or until the vegetables are tender.

Home-made Chicken Stock

Chicken stock is simple to make and well worth the effort. The outside, coarse sticks of celery are perfect for this recipe.

Makes about 600 ml (1 pint)

1 chicken carcass or a selection of chicken bones
1 unpeeled onion, quartered
2 carrots, sliced
1 celery stick, sliced
2–3 bay leaves
1 tablespoon chopped herbs (such as parsley, thyme, rosemary, sage) or ¼–½ teaspoon dried mixed herbs
1 tablespoon (or more) jelly left over from roasting a chicken (optional)
pepper
pinch of low-sodium salt

1 Place the chicken carcass or bones in a large saucepan with the vegetables and herbs and the jelly, if using. Season with pepper and low-sodium salt.

2 Cover with water, bring to the boil and skim off the scum that rises to the surface. Reduce the heat, cover and simmer for 30 minutes–1 hour, topping up with a little boiling water from time to time, if necessary.

3 Strain the stock and discard the vegetables and bones. The stock can be stored in the refrigerator for up to 3 days. It also freezes well.

Braised Vegetables with Dill and Mustard

For this recipe you need 500 g (1 lb) or as much as you can eat of your favourite leafy green vegetable, for example Brussels sprouts, spring greens, baby spinach, broccoli or green beans.

Serves 1

500 g (1 lb) leafy green vegetables
300 ml (½ pint) Home-made Chicken or Vegetable Stock (see left), or ½ vegetable stock cube dissolved in 300 ml (½ pint) hot water
1 teaspoon chopped dill
2 teaspoons wholegrain mustard
salt and pepper

1 Prepare the vegetables according to type while you warm the stock in a large saucepan.

2 When the stock is boiling, add the vegetables to the pan, reduce the heat and simmer for 5–10 minutes, until just crisp or tender. Transfer the vegetables to a serving plate with a slotted spoon. Stir the dill and mustard into the stock and season with salt and pepper to taste. Pour the stock over the vegetables.

variation

Make Vegetable Stock in the same way as chicken, but omit the carcass or bones and the jelly.

Melon and Grape Salad

You can use any variety of melon, except watermelon, for this salad.

Serves 1

1 large slice of melon
1 handful of black or white seedless
    grapes, halved
juice of ½ lime
1 teaspoon clear honey
1–2 mint or lemon balm sprigs,
    finely shredded

1 Cut the melon into chunks and tip into a bowl with its juice.

2 Add the grapes, lime juice, honey and herbs. Mix well and chill before serving.

Mango Smoothie

Serves 1

1 large ripe mango
300 ml (½ pint) freshly squeezed orange juice
mint leaves, to decorate

1 Halve the mango and scoop the flesh and any juice into a food processor or blender. Add the orange juice and blend for 1 minute.

2 Pour into a glass. Add a few mint leaves to decorate and serve with a straw.

tip

To prepare a mango, hold it upright on a board. Slice the flesh from either side of the stone. Trim off the flesh still clinging to the stone. Score the flesh of the two large pieces in a diamond pattern, without cutting through the skin. Turn the skin inside out and slice the flesh away from it.

Primavera Stir-Fry

Serves 1

100–200 ml (3½–7 fl oz) Home-made
 Chicken or Vegetable Stock (see page 37)
 or water
2 rosemary sprigs
75 g (3 oz) green beans
1 small handful of broccoli florets
1 small handful of cauliflower florets
125 g (4 oz) mushrooms
6–8 cherry tomatoes, halved
3–4 spring onions, chopped
1 tablespoon balsamic vinegar
small handful of basil leaves, torn into pieces

1 Heat the stock or water with the rosemary
sprigs in a large wok or frying pan until it
comes to the boil.

2 Meanwhile, clean and roughly chop
the beans, broccoli, cauliflower and
mushrooms. Add to the boiling stock or
water. Cover the pan and shake gently from
time to time to ensure the vegetables don't
stick to the pan or burn.

3 Test for tenderness after 5 minutes. Add
the cherry tomatoes, spring onions and
balsamic vinegar and cook for 1 minute,
stirring. Serve scattered with the basil.

Spicy Baked Potato

Try to make the time to bake the potato in a hot oven, as oven-baked potatoes are much crisper and tastier than microwaved ones.

Serves 1

1 large baking potato
15 g (½ oz) low-fat butter replacement
spicy low-calorie, 'no-added sugar' tomato
   salsa, to serve (optional)
salt and pepper

1 Wash and dry the potato then prick the skin with a sharp knife. Place directly on the shelf of a preheated oven, 200°C (400°F), Gas Mark 6, and bake for 1–1½ hours.

2 When cooked, slit the potato in half lengthways and scrape the potato flesh out of the skins. Mash with the low-fat butter replacement, salt and plenty of pepper.

3 Return the mashed potato to the skins and serve dressed with a little low-calorie, 'no-added sugar' tomato salsa, if you like.

Warm Rice Salad with Lemon, Garlic and Herbs

This recipe uses the total amount of rice allowed for Day 7 (see page 36). Make up this salad and eat half of it. Use the remainder as the basis for the Oriental Risotto (see right). Divide the broccoli into small equal-size florets to ensure they cook evenly.

Serves 1

65–75 g (2½–3 oz) brown rice
about 450 ml (¾ pint) Home-made Chicken or
   Vegetable Stock (see page 37)
2 carrots, grated
1 handful of broccoli florets
grated rind of ½ lemon
1 small garlic clove, chopped
1 tablespoon chopped flat leaf parsley

1 Cook the rice in the stock until tender, but with a little bite. This will take about 20 minutes, so 5 minutes before the rice is ready, stir in the grated carrot and broccoli. Meanwhile, mix together the lemon rind, garlic and parsley.

2 Drain the rice and vegetables when cooked, reserving any cooking juices for soup, and divide into 2 portions. Set one aside for use in the Oriental Risotto. Serve the the remainder scattered with the lemon rind and herb mixture.

Oriental Risotto

Serves 1

leftover Warm Rice Salad with Lemon, Garlic
   and Herbs (see left)
50 ml (2 fl oz) clear stock or water
1 teaspoon Chinese five-spice powder
1 handful of cherry tomatoes, halved
1 handful of button or oyster mushrooms,
   halved
1 heaped tablespoon grated mooli
1 teaspoon seasoned rice wine vinegar
soy sauce, to taste

1 Heat the leftover rice salad gently in a little stock or water with the five-spice powder. When warmed through, stir in the tomatoes, mushrooms and grated mooli.

2 Stir well and cook gently for 2 minutes. Stir in the rice wine vinegar. Season to taste with soy sauce and serve.

- ▶ Stabilizer principles

- ▶ Buying and cooking tips

- ▶ Eating philosophy

- ▶ Basic Stabilizer Plan with guidelines,
  daily allowances and Stabilizer
  Plan breakfasts

- ▶ The 14-day Basic Stabilizer Plan

- ▶ Recipes

4 The Fat-burner Foods Basic Stabilizer Plan

stabilizer principles

There are four possible Stabilizer Plans, each designed to establish your weight at its new level. They include three meals a day and snacks derived from a wide range of healthy foods, to give you a rest from the Rapid Fat Loss Plan, and ideas for menu choices in future. You won't go hungry on the FBF Stabilizer Plan, any more than on the FBF Rapid Fat Loss Plan.

The Basic Stabilizer Plan outlined in this chapter comprises fine, fresh foods at realistic prices to suit all the family. There are three other Stabilizer Plans – Luxury, Vegetarian and Entertaining (see Chapter 5). Choose the one that suits you and your lifestyle. You could replace one whole day from one plan with another, although the best option is to stick to the complete two-week programme of whichever Stabilizer Plan you have chosen.

The majority of the foods in each of the Stabilizer Plans are fat-burners. Although many people do lose a little weight during this fortnight, fat-burning is not its dedicated purpose. The important thing is not to lose patience but to enjoy all the delicious foods you are free to eat over the next two weeks, knowing that the 14 further fat-burning days that follow will kickstart your body's metabolism into losing more fat should you need to do so. Continue weighing yourself daily while you're learning to replace your old eating habits with healthier choices. You will soon discover how much carbohydrate you can safely eat, for instance, without the weight piling back on.

Whichever version of the FBF Stabilizer Plan you choose, you will see that it has points in common with the Rapid Fat Loss Plan. The emphasis is on fresh, raw or lightly cooked fruit and vegetables, wholegrain carbohydrates and sources of protein with high fat-burning potential. The plans are low in fat and refined carbohydrates. Each of the Stabilizer Plans:

• Utilizes the grazing method – eating small meals and snacking throughout the day to raise the metabolic rate.
• Is rich in essential nutrients, such as antioxidants, to boost immunity, energy and mood.
• Contains much natural plant fibre, which provides that satisfying feeling of fullness and maintains healthy blood sugar and insulin levels.
• Is rich in foods with reputed special fat-burning properties.
• Ensures that weight lost stays lost and the health risks of obesity become a thing of the past.

buying and cooking tips

As for the FBF Rapid Fat Loss Plan, organic foods are the preferred choice, especially for fresh fruit and vegetables and good-quality cuts of meat.

Remove all skin and fat from meat and poultry before cooking. Cook meat, poultry and fish by grilling, boiling, baking, steaming or stir-frying in a little water or broth or a teaspoon of olive oil as described in the recipes. Do not fry or braise in oil, and ideally do not roast these foods unless *all* visible fat is removed and slices of the meat are wiped free of fat using absorbent kitchen paper. All yogurt, cottage cheese, fromage frais and crème fraîche should be low-fat versions. Eggs should ideally be free-range; they may be boiled, poached or scrambled using a little low-fat butter replacement from the daily allowance. If using soya products, choose soya-derived meat and dairy substitutes with 'no added' fat, starch or sugar.

In most of the recipes very little oil is used for 'frying' the vegetables so the pan needs to be covered so that they cook largely in their own steam. Rinse ingredients preserved in oil, such as canned fish or bottled peppers, before using.

eating philosophy

The often-quoted saying of Confucius, 'Everyone eats, but few know flavour', is as valid as ever. How often do we pause long enough while we are eating to allow our food to stimulate more than our (fleeting) sense of taste? Food has texture, temperature and aroma and can certainly be made pleasing to the sight with little trouble. Some foods and drinks even have their own 'music', as the advertisers of certain fizzy drinks, toasted rice cereal and popcorn were not slow to exploit.

Have you ever listened to the slow bubble of a thick, rich stew or noticed the slow, deep 'plop' of a simmering pan of real oatmeal porridge? What about the tempting sizzle of flambéed foods or the satisfying crunch of freshly made toast? You might think all this is a little over the top, but reflect on the fact that if you have overeaten in times of trouble or boredom in the past, you need all the sensuous props possible to help keep you on the right path of permanent weight loss.

basic stabilizer plan

The Basic Stabilizer Plan will suit you if you wish to keep within your normal budget and provide meals the whole family can enjoy. None of the recipes is expensive or complicated to make, relying, as they do, on ingredients you probably already have in your storecupboard.

Some suggestions can be varied a little according to taste and what ingredients are available. Runner beans for instance can be substituted for Brussels sprouts or spinach, while coley and 'rock salmon' make as tasty a fish pie as plaice, cod, haddock or whiting.

The fat-burning potential of the ingredients is mentioned in many of the recipes to help you remember them. Although the recipes provide ingredient quantities, many of them can be altered to suit your individual preferences. The most important thing is that you get used to eating sensibly and enjoyably, using and trusting your own judgement.

Basic Stabilizer Plan Guidelines

DO

✔ Follow the eating plan. You can omit a food you dislike, but be careful to replace it with a close nutritional equivalent: for example you can use the same weight of lean pork, veal or fresh or thawed frozen white fish instead of chicken in Lemon Chicken Stir-Fry (Day 3). It's also worth comparing calorie counts when substituting foods – always read labels.

✔ Do eat your soup, or snack on vegetables from the negative calorie foods list (see page 27), whenever you feel hungry.

✔ Keep 'grazing', that is eat small meals and snacks every 3–4 hours.

✔ Drink at least 8 large (300 ml/½ pint) glasses of plain, bottled or filtered water daily, plus herbal teas, tea and coffee, if you wish, using milk from your daily allowance.

✔ Use only the recommended dressings for salads and other recipes.

✔ Continue to weigh yourself daily and record your weight.

✔ Remember your goal and the promises you have made to yourself and renew them daily.

✔ Steer clear of alcohol, soft drinks and sweeteners.

Daily Allowance

- Negative calorie vegetables (see page 27) – as much as you want.
- Fat-burning Soup (see page 36) – as much and as often as you like.
- Two pieces of fruit from negative calories food list (see page 27) – this is in addition to any fruit listed in daily menus.
- 600 ml (1 pint) skimmed milk or 300 ml (½ pint) semi-skimmed milk or 2 x 200 g (7 oz) cartons of low-fat natural or flavoured yogurt or low-fat fromage frais.
- 15 g (½ oz) low-fat butter replacement (such as one of the cholesterol-lowering spreads).

Stabilizer Plan Breakfasts

The breakfast options are the same, whichever Stabilizer Plan you are following. There are three options so you can vary your breakfast over the 14 days.

BREAKFAST 1

- Small glass (150–175 ml/ 5–6 fl oz) of tomato or other vegetable juice, such as carrot juice or Carrot and Celery Juice (see page 59).
- 1 portion of fresh fruit (such as 1 apple, 1–2 satsumas or 5–6 strawberries), chopped into 200 ml (7 fl oz) low-fat natural yogurt and sprinkled with 1 dessertspoon of wheatgerm.
- If still hungry: 1 slice of toasted/untoasted wholemeal bread with a little low-fat butter replacement from daily allowance, yeast extract or reduced-sugar marmalade or jam.

BREAKFAST 2

- Small glass (150–175 ml/ 5–6 fl oz) of unsweetened natural fruit juice (NOTE: Check the label – 'fruit drinks' invariably have sugar added).
- 2 wholewheat cereal bisks with milk from the daily allowance.
- 1 portion of fresh fruit (such as 1 apple or orange, or 2 satsumas).
- If still hungry: 1 slice of toasted/untoasted wholemeal bread with a little low-fat butter replacement from daily allowance, yeast extract or reduced-sugar marmalade or jam.

BREAKFAST 3

- Citrus segments and juice, for example ½ grapefruit, 1 orange, 1 small can of mandarin oranges in natural juice, mixed with 1 chopped banana and 1 dessertspoon of toasted sesame seeds.
- Scrambled egg made with 1 medium or large egg and milk from daily allowance, plus 1 teaspoon low-fat butter replacement from daily allowance, served on 1 slice of toasted wholemeal bread.

The 14-Day Basic Stabilizer Plan

	DAY 1 & DAY 8	DAY 2 & DAY 9	DAY 3 & DAY 10
BREAKFAST	• One of the three breakfast options available (see page 47).	• One of the three breakfast options available (see page 47).	• One of the three breakfast options available (see page 47).
LUNCH	• Quick Tomato Soup (see page 50). • Tuna and cress sandwich (tuna in brine, drained and mixed with cress, between 2 slices of wholemeal bread spread with low-fat butter replacement from daily allowance). • 1 piece of fruit if still hungry (or save for mid-afternoon snack).	• Eggs Florentine (see page 51). • 1 slice of wholemeal bread (optional). • 6–8 plump presoaked dried apricots with 3–4 walnut halves or 2 Brazil nuts.	• Coleslaw with Peanuts (see page 50). • 1 plain bagel • 2 peeled and sliced kiwi fruit topped with 1 tablespoon of natural low-fat yogurt and 1 dessertspoon of pumpkin seeds.
DINNER	• Creamy Fish Pie (see page 54). • Spring greens or spinach. • 2–3 tablespoons low-fat yogurt ice-cream, plus chopped fresh fruit (optional).	• Spiced Beef with Apricots (see page 56). • Vegetables and 1–2 boiled potatoes mashed with milk from daily allowance. • Baked Vanilla Custard (see page 59).	• Lemon Chicken Stir-Fry (see page 57). • 200 ml (7 fl oz) low-fat apricot yogurt mixed with 2 chopped fresh or presoaked dried apricots.

DAY 4 & DAY 11	DAY 5 & DAY 12	DAY 6 & DAY 13	DAY 7 & DAY 14
• One of the three breakfast options available (see page 47).	• One of the three breakfast options available (see page 47).	• One of the three breakfast options available (see page 47).	• One of the three breakfast options available (see page 47).
• Seafood and Tomatoes on Granary (see page 52). • 1 apple.	• Spicy Lentil Soup (see page 53). • Salad sandwich (optional), made using 2 slices of wholemeal bread and low-fat butter replacement from daily allowance. • 100–200 ml (3½–7 fl oz) low-fat yogurt (optional).	• Toasted cheese sandwich (2 slices of light rye bread spread lightly with low-fat butter replacement from daily allowance and 50–75 g (2–3 oz) low-fat cottage cheese with chives mixed with 2 teaspoons of grated Parmesan cheese). • 3 fresh plums or greengages.	• As much fresh fruit salad as you like, using at least 1 citrus fruit (e.g. grapefruit or orange), 1 apple and/or pear, berries and soft fruits in season. Serve with 2 tablespoons low-fat cottage cheese mixed with 1 tablespoon sesame seeds, preferably toasted.
• Kidneys Courtesan with Jamaican Cabbage (see page 56). • 1–2 boiled potatoes • 2–3 tablespoons of chilled stewed apple, flavoured with a little cardamom.	• Salad Niçoise (see page 55). • 100–200 g (3½–7 oz) low-fat fromage frais mixed with 2 peeled and chopped kiwi fruits.	• Orange Pork (see page 58). • Green vegetables, such as Brussels sprouts or spinach. • 3–4 tablespoons boiled brown rice. • 1 handful of fresh cherries and 5–6 whole shelled almonds.	• Quick Fish Tartare (see page 55). • 1–2 mashed floury potatoes. • Green beans. • 3–4 tablespoons fresh chopped fruit topped with a little low-fat natural yogurt and 1 teaspoon brown sugar. Glaze under a preheated grill until caramelized.

Quick Tomato Soup

Serves 2

350–450 ml (12–15 fl oz) Home-made
Chicken or Vegetable Stock (see page 37)
6 tomatoes, chopped, or 400 g (13 oz) can
chopped tomatoes
1 tablespoon sun-dried tomato paste
1 small onion, finely chopped
75–125 g (3–4 oz) leftover negative calorie
vegetables (see page 27) that have been
cooked without fat or oil (optional)
2 oregano or marjoram sprigs or ½ teaspoon
dried oregano
dash of Worcestershire sauce or pinch of
chilli powder
4 teaspoons natural yogurt and basil leaves,
to garnish

1 Heat the home-made stock. Add the
tomatoes and their juice, tomato paste,
onion, leftover vegetables, if using, and
oregano or marjoram.

2 Bring just to the boil, then lower the heat
and simmer for 5–10 minutes, stirring
occasionally. Add Worcestershire sauce or
chilli powder to taste and blend lightly in a
blender or food processor, if liked. Serve
swirled with yogurt and scattered with
basil leaves.

Coleslaw with Peanuts

The juice from the freshly grated
vegetables keeps the coleslaw
beautifully moist, and the onion
provides a real kick, so there is no
need for any dressing other than
some freshly ground black pepper.
However, if liked you could mix a
dressing with 2 teaspoons of olive
oil, 1 teaspoon of clear honey and
1 teaspoon of lemon juice.

Serves 1

75–125 g (3–4 oz) fresh cabbage heart,
finely shredded
½–1 small onion, finely grated
1 carrot, finely grated
1 dessertspoon sultanas
50 g (2 oz) unsalted or dry roasted peanuts
black pepper

1 Mix together the cabbage, onion and
carrot in a large bowl.

2 Stir in the sultanas and peanuts and
season to taste with black pepper.

Eggs Florentine

The eggs provide protein while the spinach provides iron, calcium and magnesium for fat-burning, as well as offering negative calories. Use frozen spinach if fresh is unavailable.

Serves 1

100–200 g (3½–7 oz) fresh spinach
1 tablespoon water
1 teaspoon vinegar
1 large or 2 small eggs
freshly grated nutmeg
salt and pepper

1 Wash the spinach and place in a large saucepan with the water. Cover and cook over a medium heat for 1–2 minutes, until wilted. Season to taste.

2 When soft, cut through the spinach roughly with a sharp knife and transfer to a warmed serving plate.

3 Meanwhile, set a frying pan on the hob and pour in boiling water to a depth of about 2.5 cm (1 inch). Keep the water at a gentle rolling boil. Add the vinegar to hold the eggs together. Crack each egg into a saucer and slip it gently into the boiling water. Cook just long enough to set the white while the yolk remains runny. Remove the poached egg with a slotted spoon and slide on to the spinach. Season with plenty of nutmeg, salt and pepper.

Seafood and Tomatoes on Granary

You should have no problem pleasing your family with today's lunch menu of cockles and winkles. Their very image harks back to a kinder, slower era when a small carton of what we now call 'seafood', bought from a fishmonger's stall at a market and eaten with bread and butter and vinegar, was a real treat. Many people today have never even tasted them.

Serves 1

125 g (4 oz) shelled or 250 g (8 oz) unshelled cooked mixed shellfish (such as winkles, whelks, cockles)
malt vinegar, to taste
pepper
To serve:
1 hunk of granary bread
low-fat butter replacement, to spread
2 sun-ripened tomatoes (optional)

1 Flick off the little brown protective shields from the winkles and whelks using a cocktail stick (cockles come undefended), then delve into the interior of the shell for the delicious prize.

2 Dip the shellfish in malt vinegar and a little pepper, and eat with a hunk of fresh granary bread, spread with a scraping of low-fat butter replacement. A couple of sun-ripened tomatoes go well with this, too.

Spicy Lentil Soup

Don't be surprised when the rest of your family demand to try this extremely quick and tasty soup on smelling it! You do not have to soak red lentils before use. They can be stored in airtight jars or other containers for up to a year.

Serves 1–2

50–75 g (2–3 oz) red lentils
1 onion, very thinly sliced
1 garlic clove, crushed (optional)
350–450 ml (12–15 fl oz) Home-made Chicken or Vegetable
  Stock (see page 37)
½ teaspoon medium curry paste
lemon juice, to taste
low-fat crème fraîche and torn coriander leaves, to garnish

1 Rinse the lentils and place in a saucepan with the onion and garlic, if using, and the stock.

2 Bring to the boil, then reduce the heat; add the curry paste, stir and cover. The lentils and the onion take about 20 minutes to soften – top up with boiling water if the volume becomes too reduced.

3 When cooked, purée the soup in a food processor or blender and add a little lemon juice to taste. Turn into soup bowls, swirl with crème fraîche and scatter with coriander leaves.

Creamy Fish Pie

The fish provides good healthy protein for fat-burning; the corn or baked beans are low-GI carbohydrates, and the milk provides the minerals calcium and magnesium for energy and for strong teeth and bones.

Serves 1

1–2 potatoes, peeled and cut into chunks
125–175 g (4–6 oz) white fish fillet (such as coley, rock salmon, cod)
4–5 tablespoons full-cream milk
125 g (4 oz) button mushrooms, sliced (optional)
2–3 tablespoons canned 'no-added sugar' sweetcorn or baked beans
white pepper or freshly grated nutmeg, to taste

1 Cook the potatoes in a saucepan of boiling water until tender.

2 Meanwhile, place the fish on a large heatproof plate suitable for steaming or for use in a microwave. Cover with a little of the milk and season with pepper and/or grated nutmeg.

3 To steam the fish, set the plate over a saucepan of boiling water. Cover and steam gently for 5–6 minutes or until cooked. To microwave the fish, cover it and cook on medium power, checking frequently, until cooked – it takes about 2 minutes per fillet depending upon the thickness of the fish and the oven wattage.

4 Place the mushrooms in a small pan with the sweetcorn. Cover and cook gently for a few minutes. Strain off the liquid and keep the vegetables warm.

5 Place the fish with its cooking liquid in an ovenproof dish, and add a little more milk if it looks dry. Top with the mushroom and sweetcorn mixture.

6 Drain the potatoes then mash them with the remaining milk to a creamy consistency. Season with nutmeg and pile the potato on top of the fish, mushrooms and sweetcorn. Brown under a preheated grill and serve.

Salad Niçoise

Serves 1

¼ Cos lettuce, coarsely chopped

3–4 cherry tomatoes, halved

6 spring onions, chopped

5 cm (2 inch) piece of cucumber, left unpeeled and chopped

1 large hard-boiled egg, quartered

4 canned anchovy fillets in olive oil, drained, olive oil reserved

4 pitted black olives

lemon juice, to taste

black pepper

To serve:

1 wholegrain bagel

125–175 g (4–6 oz) grilled fresh tuna steak or tuna canned in brine, drained (optional)

1 Assemble all the ingredients and arrange on a plate or in a salad bowl. Dress the salad with a little oil from the can of anchovies, a good squeeze of lemon juice and some black pepper.

2 Serve with a wholegrain bagel and, if you want more protein, a grilled fresh tuna steak or some drained, canned tuna.

Quick Fish Tartare

This is ideal served with plain mashed floury potatoes as they soak up the delicious cooking liquid.

Serves 1

175–250 g (6–8 oz) cod fillet

1 teaspoon olive oil

1 teaspoon lemon juice

3–4 parsley or fennel sprigs, chopped

1 gherkin, chopped

6–8 capers, drained, rinsed and chopped

salt and pepper

1 Place the cod on a large heatproof plate suitable for steaming or for use in a microwave. Spoon over the oil and lemon juice and scatter with the herbs, gherkin and capers. Season lightly.

2 To steam the cod, set the plate over a saucepan of boiling water. Cover and steam gently for 7–9 minutes or until cooked through and the flesh flakes easily. Alternatively, to microwave the fish, cover it and cook on medium power for about 3–4 minutes, checking frequently until cooked through and the flesh flakes easily.

Kidneys Courtesan with Jamaican Cabbage

This recipe is so called because the kidneys are saucy, bold and blushing – cooked to the point of pink succulence and not a jot more. If you prefer, replace the kidneys with 175 g (6 oz) skinless, boneless chicken breast.

Serves 1

2 teaspoons olive oil
1 onion, thinly sliced
2 lamb's kidneys, skinned, cored and halved
½–1 cm (¼–½ inch) piece of fresh root ginger, grated or very finely sliced
dash of Worcestershire sauce
1 large handful of shredded cabbage
1 tablespoon lemon juice
white pepper and low-sodium salt substitute

1 Heat the oil in a large frying pan, add the sliced onion and its juices. Cook, tightly covered, until soft. Add the kidneys, ginger and Worcestershire sauce and cook, covered, for 4–5 minutes over a low to medium heat.

2 Remove the kidneys from the pan with a slotted spoon, transfer to a plate and keep warm.

3 Add the cabbage and lemon juice to the pan, and cook over a low to medium heat, stirring occasionally. Add a little hot water if the cabbage seems too dry, and season with white pepper and salt substitute. Stir in the cooked kidneys and their juices and serve immediately.

Spiced Beef with Apricots

Serves 1

1 teaspoon olive oil
1 onion, thinly sliced
2–3 garlic cloves, crushed or finely chopped
1 cinnamon stick, halved
75–125 g (3–4 oz) good-quality minced lean beef or chicken
1 leek, sliced
2 apricots, peeled, pitted and chopped
1 teaspoon grated orange rind
juice of 1 orange
2 teaspoons finely chopped fresh root ginger
salt and pepper

1 Heat the olive oil in a pan. Add the onion, garlic and cinnamon and gently fry, covered, until brown.

2 Add the minced beef or chicken to the pan and cook gently, stirring constantly, for 5 minutes.

3 When the meat is brown and cooked through, add the leek, apricots, grated orange rind, orange juice and ginger. Cover, and cook for a further 8–10 minutes until all the vegetables are soft. Season to taste, remove and discard the cinnamon and serve.

tip

If you like liver, you could replace the mince with the same weight of thinly sliced lamb's liver for a meal loaded with iron, B vitamins and first-class protein.

Lemon Chicken Stir-Fry

Serves 1

1 teaspoon olive oil

1 small onion, finely sliced

1 large garlic clove, crushed or finely sliced

125 g (4 oz) skinless, boneless chicken breast, diced

1 dessertspoon grated lemon rind

5–6 baby corn cobs, halved diagonally

75–125 g (3–4 oz) mangetouts, diagonally sliced

1 tablespoon lemon juice

pinch of cumin

1 slice of toasted French bread or 3–4 heaped tablespoons
   boiled brown rice, to serve

1 Heat the olive oil in a frying pan or wok. Add the onion
  and garlic and cook, tightly covered, until soft.

2 Add the diced chicken, lemon rind and baby corn cobs
  and continue cooking, covered, for 5 minutes. Stir in the
mangetouts, lemon juice and cumin, cover and continue
cooking for 5 minutes more, until the chicken is cooked
right through.

3 Serve with a slice of toasted French bread or some plain
  boiled brown rice.

Orange Pork

Serves 1

125–175 g (4–6 oz) pork fillet, trimmed of fat

1 teaspoon grated orange rind

1 small garlic clove, crushed

crushed seeds from 4 cardamom pods
(optional)

1 teaspoon olive oil

juice of 1 orange

1 tablespoon low-fat crème fraîche or fromage
frais

1 handful of watercress, chopped

1 tablespoon chopped parsley

salt and pepper

To serve:

brown rice

green vegetables, such as broccoli and
mangetouts

1 Make several deep slits in the pork using a sharp knife to make pockets. Mix the orange rind, garlic, cardamom seeds, if using, and a little salt and pepper and use the mixture to fill the pockets.

2 Heat the oil in a frying pan and swirl it around to coat the base. Place the pork in the pan, cover and cook gently, turning frequently, for 10 minutes on each side until cooked through. Test by piercing the thickest piece with a knife; if the juices run clear, the pork is cooked. Remove the pork and keep warm.

3 Add the orange juice, crème fraîche or fromage frais, chopped watercress and parsley to the pan, and stir to blend with the pork juices and sediment. When heated through, pour the mixture over the pork fillet and serve with the rice and green vegetables.

Carrot and Celery Juice

This is an ideal healthy drink for breakfast if you have an electric juicer. Serve the juice as soon as it is made as some of the valuable nutrients are quickly destroyed on exposure to the air.

Serves 1

2 medium or large carrots
2 medium or large celery sticks
dash of Tabasco sauce (optional)

1 Cut the carrots and celery into large chunks and pass through a juicer. Stir in the Tabasco, if using. Serve immediately.

variation

Substitute 1 ripe green apple for the celery sticks to make a delicious carrot and apple juice.

Baked Vanilla Custard

The eggs and milk provide fat-burning protein, while the organic real vanilla extract is sheer heaven for the taste buds.

Serves 3–4

600 ml (1 pint) semi-skimmed milk
3 eggs
1 teaspoon clear honey
3–4 drops pure organic vanilla extract
freshly grated nutmeg, to taste
stewed tart fruit (such as Victoria plums or damsons), to serve

1 Warm the milk in a saucepan. Beat the eggs with the honey and vanilla extract in a bowl. Pour in the milk, whisking well. Strain into an ovenproof dish or 3–4 ramekins.

2 Place in a roasting tin containing 1 cm (½ inch) cold water and bake in a preheated oven, 160°C (325°F), Gas Mark 3, for about 20 minutes, until set.

3 Serve hot, warm or cold with a little stewed tart fruit.

▶ **Luxury Stabilizer Plan – and 14-day chart**

▶ **Vegetarian Stabilizer Plan – and 14-day chart**

▶ **Entertaining Stabilizer Plan – and 14 day chart**

▶ **Recipes**

5 Three Alternative Stabilizer Plans

luxury stabilizer plan

The luxury plan will appeal to you if you enjoy cooking and eating fine foods. Not all recipes in this section are expensive to make and none of them is complicated. Chicken with Winter Vegetables, for instance, is a simple dish of chicken cooked slowly with delicious winter vegetables.

Whiting Stoker takes only minutes to prepare, while Strawberries with Crème Fraîche and Grand Marnier combines luscious strawberries with orange flavours. The guidelines, daily allowances and the breakfast options are the same as for the Basic Stabilizer Plan (see pages 46 and 47).

vegetarian stabilizer plan

This version of the plan will suit non-meat eaters who eat eggs and dairy products, but it can be adapted to suit vegans.

As always, do follow the eating plan. You can omit a food you dislike, but be sensible about any substitutions you make.

The guidelines, daily allowances and the breakfast options are the same as for the Basic Stabilizer Plan (see pages 46 and 47). However, vegetarians will want to make their Fat-burning Soup with vegetable stock. Vegans should replace dairy products and eggs with the appropriate alternatives.

remember

Do follow the eating plan. Omit a food you dislike, but replace it with a close nutritional equivalent. Always substitute like for like, in similar quantities. It's also worth comparing calorie counts. In addition, keep 'grazing' – small meals and snacks every 3–4 hours – drink plenty of water and eat the Fat-burning Soup (see page 36) or negative calorie vegetables (see page 27) whenever you feel hungry.

entertaining stabilizer plan

Welcome to the Entertaining Stabilizer Plan, the third alternative FBF Stabilizer Plan designed to establish your weight at its new level. Three meals a day plus snacks give you a break from the FBF Rapid Fat Loss Plan, and the menus, which include a wide selection of fat-burning foods, provide numerous ideas for healthier eating.

Specifically, the Entertaining Stabilizer will help you maintain your weight loss (and perhaps lose a little more) when cooking for guests or maybe on holiday – situations known to shake the resolve of the most committed dieters, who pile back the weight they've worked hard to lose.

Your commitment and effort are still necessary! No magical formula can free you to feast on junk foods without regaining the weight you have lost. But your fortnight on the FBF Rapid Fat Loss Plan should have left you lighter, fitter, more energetic and even more determined to succeed than ever. Achieving your target weight by melting stubborn fat is the first priority of the FBF Weight Loss Programme. The second priority is to help you maintain your new weight from a knowledge of foods with fat-burning potential.

As always, the emphasis is on fresh raw or lightly cooked fruit and vegetables, wholegrain carbohydrates and proteins with high fat-burning potential. Few of the recipes are expensive or complicated and many of the meals are ones the whole family can enjoy. All the same, eating out and entertaining generally involve foods outside the scope of the average week's catering and are regarded as treats.

More economical versions of many of the recipes will undoubtedly spring to mind, and you can safely follow them, provided you always replace like with like. For example, you could replace one type of white fish with another, pumpernickel with some other type of wholegrain bread, or low-fat cottage cheese with low-fat fromage frais or half its weight of reduced-fat hard cheese such as Cheddar.

The advice, guidelines, daily allowances and breakfast options are the same as for the Basic Stabilizer Plan (see pages 46 and 47).

The 14-Day Luxury Stabilizer Plan

	DAY 1 & DAY 8	DAY 2 & DAY 9	DAY 3 & DAY 10
BREAKFAST	• One of the three breakfast options available (see page 47).	• One of the three breakfast options available (see page 47).	• One of the three breakfast options available (see page 47).
LUNCH	• Avocado and Prawns on Rye (see page 72). • 1 peach or 2 ripe dessert plums.	• Smoked Cod's Roe with Melba Toast (see page 73). • 3–4 fresh apricots or 50 g (2 oz) dried apricots, soaked overnight.	• Smoked Trout and Rainbow Salad (see page 80). • 1 handful of black or white grapes.
DINNER	• Fat-burner Steak Diane (see page 86). • Steamed broccoli. • Small/medium baked potato topped with a little Farmhouse Dressing (see page 80). • 1 large slice of fresh pineapple or 1 sliced banana topped with a little low-fat natural yogurt.	• Herb-crusted Lamb with Spring Greens (see page 88). • 1 boiled potato mashed with a little skimmed milk from daily allowance. • Lemon jelly made with 300 ml (½ pint) water, served with 1 chopped apple.	• Mixed Grill (see page 89). • Salad of watercress, orange and mint (see page 76). • 3–4 tablespoons boiled brown rice mixed with 1 tablespoon lemon or lime juice and 2 tablespoons chopped parsley. • Strawberries with Crème Fraiche and Grand Marnier (see page 101).

DAY 4 & DAY 11	DAY 5 & DAY 12	DAY 6 & DAY 13	DAY 7 & DAY 14
• One of the three breakfast options available (see page 47).	• One of the three breakfast options available (see page 47).	• One of the three breakfast options available (see page 47).	• One of the three breakfast options available (see page 47).
• Wilted Spinach with Eggs and Herb Butter (see page 83). • An astringent dessert after the rich main course, perhaps Minty Citrus Replete (see page 101).	• Courgette Stuffed Mushrooms (see page 84). • 1 slice of wholemeal bread. • Peppery salad of watercress, rocket and radishes (see page 77). • 6 plump presoaked dried prunes with 10–12 macadamia nuts.	• Chicken Antipasto (see page 70). • 2 kiwi fruits.	• Fresh Sardine Salad and Citrus Mint Tabbouleh (see page 74). • Persimmon Cream (see page 103).
• Chicken and Winter Vegetables (see page 89). • 1–2 boiled potatoes. • Green vegetables such as Brussels sprouts, spinach or broccoli. • Fruit Fanfare (see page 102).	• Seafood Vermicelli with Tomato and Mushroom Sauce (see page 95). • Walnut and Honey Yogurt (see page 102).	• Whiting Stoker with Green Beans and Cayenne Potato (see page 96). • Fresh fruit salad made with ½ grapefruit, 2–3 slices of pineapple and 1 pear, and a little ground cinnamon.	• Spiced Turkey on a Bed of Potato (see page 91). • Broad beans. • Traditional Baked Apple (see page 103).

The 14-Day Vegetarian Stabilizer Plan

	DAY 1 & DAY 8	DAY 2 & DAY 9	DAY 3 & DAY 10
BREAKFAST	• One of the three breakfast options available (see page 47).	• One of the three breakfast options available (see page 47).	• One of the three breakfast options available (see page 47).
LUNCH	• Celery and carrot sticks and broccoli spears served with 2 tablespoons of low-calorie mayonnaise, for dipping. • 2–3 crispbreads. • 1 piece of fruit such as an apple or orange.	• Cottage Cheese Salsa on Toast (see page 72). • 2–3 mandarins.	• Viva Tomatoes on Toast (see page 75). • 15–20 black or white grapes.
DINNER	• Vegetarian Sausages with Tomato and Herb Mash (see page 97). • 100–200 ml (3½–7 fl oz) of natural low-fat yogurt mixed with 2 teaspoons of honeycomb and a little finely chopped fresh root ginger.	• Flageolet and Mushroom Savoury (see page 100). • Brussels sprouts. • 1 slice of wholemeal toast. • Grilled Pears with Oatmeal and Raspberry Cream (see page 104).	•Herb Omelette (see page 85). • Small baked potato. • Salad of celery, apple and lettuce. • Lemon jelly made with 300 ml (½ pint) water, served with a small can of mandarins.

DAY 4 & DAY 11	DAY 5 & DAY 12	DAY 6 & DAY 13	DAY 7 & DAY 14
• One of the three breakfast options available (see page 47).	• One of the three breakfast options available (see page 47).	• One of the three breakfast options available (see page 47).	• One of the three breakfast options available (see page 47).
• Courgette Stuffed Mushrooms (see page 84). • 1 slice of toasted sourdough bread. • Tomato and Spring Onion Salad (see page 73). • 125–175 g (4–6 oz) of strawberries.	• Warm Bean Salad with Fresh Herbs (see page 78). • 1 thick slice of wholemeal bread. • 75–125 g (3–4 oz) raspberries drizzled with a little clear honey, if liked.	• Slimmers' Coleslaw (see page 81). • 1 slice of sourdough or barley bread. • 100–200 ml (3½–7 fl oz) of vanilla-flavoured or natural low-fat yogurt.	• Bean Sprouts with Soy and Ginger (see page 84). • 1 hunk of soft wholemeal bread or 2–3 tablespoons boiled brown rice. • 75–125 g (3–4 oz) canned fruit in natural juice.
• Tomato and Courgette Bake (see page 98). • Chicory, Orange and Black Olive Salad (see page 75). • 100–200 ml (3½–7 fl oz) of low-fat fruit yogurt served with fresh chopped fruit.	• Stuffed Tomatoes (see page 81). • Artichoke, Endive and Green Herb Salad (see page 76) or Chinese cabbage sliced and gently cooked with 1 garlic clove in a little vegetable stock. • Arabian Apricots (see page 106).	• Steamed Vegetables with Guacamole Topping (see page 99). • 1 slice of melon topped with a spoon of chilled low-fat fromage frais, plus 1 dessertspoon of melon liqueur (optional) poured over just before serving.	• Sautéed Artichokes with Brazil Nuts (see page 99). • Steamed baby courgettes and freshly cooked and chopped spring greens. • Traditional Baked Apple (see page 103).

The 14-Day Entertaining Stabilizer Plan

	DAY 1 & DAY 8	DAY 2 & DAY 9	DAY 3 & DAY 10
BREAKFAST	• One of the three breakfast options available (see page 47).	• One of the three breakfast options available (see page 47).	• One of the three breakfast options available (see page 47).
LUNCH	• Sautéed Monkfish with Green Gem Salad (see page 94). • 1 slice of corn bread or wholemeal bread. • 1 portion of fresh fruit such as 15 cherries or grapes.	• Jerusalem Artichoke Soup (see page 71). • 1 slice of hot crisp wholemeal toast. • Satsuma and Watercress Salad (see page 76). • 1 apple.	• Green Bean and Egg Salad (see page 79). • 1 slice of corn bread. • 1–2 scoops good-quality, reduced-calorie ice-cream.
DINNER	• Italian Chicken with Pan-Fried Vegetables (see page 91). • Lychees with Almond Junket (see page 105).	• Garlic Steak with Spring Vegetables (see page 87). • Warm Pineapple Gratin (see page 104).	• Salmon with Lemon, Parsley and Tarragon (see page 93). • Sliced tomatoes. • 1 boiled potato mashed with a little skimmed milk from daily allowance . • Apple and Blueberry Crunch (see page 107).

Don't let your resolve slip when entertaining...

As always, follow the eating plan. If you omit a food you dislike, be sure to replace it with a close nutritional equivalent: e.g. you can use lobster, prawns or white crab meat instead of fish in Sautéed Monkfish with Green Gem Salad (Day 1), or replace a particular vegetable in any of the salad recipes with any vegetables on the negative calorie foods list (see page 27). But always substitute like for like, in similar quantities. It's also worth comparing calorie counts – for example do check the fat and calorie count of various so-called 'low-fat' dairy products.

DAY 4 & DAY 11	DAY 5 & DAY 12	DAY 6 & DAY 13	DAY 7 & DAY 14
• One of the three breakfast options available (see page 47).	• One of the three breakfast options available (see page 47).	• One of the three breakfast options available (see page 47).	• One of the three breakfast options available (see page 47).
• Prawns in Brandy Cream Sauce (see page 92). • Arabian Apricots (see page 106).	• Toasted Gammon Salad Sandwich (see page 70). • 300 ml (½ pint) glass of freshly squeezed apple or carrot juice. • 1 ripe pear.	• Crab Salad (see page 82). • 1 crusty wholemeal roll.	• Truffle Eggs (see page 83). • 1 portion of fresh fruit such as ½ ugli fruit.
• Pasta with Smoked Salmon and Asparagus (see page 93). • 15 top-quality black or white grapes.	Courgette Stuffed Mushrooms (see page 84). • 1 slice of ciabatta or wholemeal bread or a baked potato. • If you wish, follow with a light protein course, such as 125–175 g (4–6 oz) of steamed or microwaved white fish, or steamed chicken breast brushed with lemon juice and served dressed with 2 teaspoons of finely grated lemon rind. • Grilled Pears with Oatmeal and Raspberry Cream (see page 104).	• Veal Schnitzel with Spinach and Brazil Nuts (see page 87). • 1 boiled potato. • Small bowl of cherries or other fresh fruit.	• Harissa Chicken with Peppers (see page 90). • Radish Rocket Salad (see page 77). • Redcurrant Glass Ceiling (see page 106).

69

Chicken Antipasto

You can roast your own red pepper if you prefer, but peppers bottled in olive oil are much more convenient for quick sandwiches. However, do make sure you drain away the oil in which they are preserved.

Serves 1

3–4 strips of antipasto red pepper in olive oil
2 tablespoons low-fat fromage frais
2–3 basil sprigs, torn into pieces (optional)
2 slices of pumpernickel bread
75 g (3 oz) cold cooked chicken, very
   thinly sliced

1 Place the strips of pepper on kitchen paper to drain away the oil in which they were preserved. Meanwhile, mix the fromage frais with the basil, if using, and spread over the slices of pumpernickel bread.

2 Top the bread with the chicken and the strips of red pepper.

Toasted Gammon Salad Sandwich

You don't need any low-fat butter replacement in this – or indeed many other – sandwiches.

Serves 2

2 thin slices of gammon, trimmed of fat
4 slices of wholemeal and poppy seed bread
prepared English mustard, to taste
2 thin slices of reduced-fat Swiss cheese (such
   as Emmental or Gruyère)
4 tablespoons mixed chopped salad vegetables
   (such as alfalfa, cherry tomatoes, unpeeled
   cucumber)

1 Lay a slice of gammon on top of each of two slices of bread, spread with mustard and top with the Swiss cheese.

2 Place under a preheated grill until the cheese bubbles, then top each with the salad vegetables and the second slice of bread. The bread mops up the vegetable and meat juices and some of the melted cheese.

variation

You could replace the strips of red pepper with other antipasto vegetables bottled in olive oil, such as mushrooms or artichoke hearts. Make sure they are well drained.

Jerusalem Artichoke Soup

This delectable soup is equally tasty served hot or chilled. Jerusalem artichokes are small knobbly tubers that are very like fresh root ginger in appearance.

Serves 3–4

500–625 g (1–1¼ lb) Jerusalem artichokes, thinly peeled and sliced
1 onion, thinly sliced
2–3 bay leaves
600 ml (1 pint) Home-made Chicken or Vegetable Stock (see page 37) or water
450–600 ml (¾–1 pint) semi-skimmed milk
1–2 tablespoons low-fat crème fraîche
cayenne pepper and chervil sprigs, to garnish

1 Place the sliced Jerusalem artichokes, onion and bay leaves in a large saucepan with the stock or water. Bring to the boil and simmer until the vegetables are tender.

2 Add about 450 ml (¾ pint) of the milk – the exact amount depends on the quantity of starch in the artichokes. Cook a little longer, then remove the bay leaves and pour the soup into a food processor or blender. Blend until smooth, adding a little of the remaining milk if necessary.

3 To serve, float a little crème fraîche on the surface of the soup, sprinkle it with cayenne pepper and garnish with chervil.

Avocado and Prawns on Rye

You hardly need a recipe for this popular open sandwich.

Serves 1

½ large ripe avocado
1–2 teaspoons lemon juice
2 slices of wholemeal rye bread, toasted
   if liked
8–10 cooked peeled prawns
black pepper
freshly grated nutmeg

1 Score the skin of the avocado half lengthways and peel it off in two strips.

2 Remove the stone and mash the avocado flesh in a bowl with the lemon juice and black pepper to taste.

3 Pile the avocado on to the rye bread or toast. Top with the prawns and a little grated nutmeg to taste.

Cottage Cheese Salsa on Toast

Serves 1

75–125 g (3–4 oz) low-fat cottage cheese
2–3 spring onions, chopped
3–4 radishes, chopped
1 tablespoon low-calorie, 'no-added sugar'
   tomato salsa
1 slice of light rye bread

1 Combine the cottage cheese with the spring onions, radishes and tomato salsa in a bowl.

2 Toast the rye bread and pile the cottage cheese mixture on top to serve.

Smoked Cod's Roe with Melba Toast

Smoked cod's roe is often used to make taramasalata, and is a delightful treat if you are fond of fish roe and a very smoky flavour.

Serves 1

1 slice of wholemeal bread
1–3 tablespoons smoked cod's roe
lemon juice, to sprinkle
small green salad of unpeeled chopped
  cucumber and crisp lettuce leaves, to serve

1 To make the melba toast, toast the slice of bread until golden brown on both sides. Wait for a few seconds until it is cool enough to handle, then place the slice flat on a work surface and, holding it down firmly with one hand, slip a sharp knife blade into the uncooked 'middle' and slice the toast horizontally into two thinner pieces. Halve the slices diagonally.

2 Toast the uncooked sides and serve the toast warm topped with the cod's roe, sprinkled with lemon juice and accompanied by a small green salad.

Tomato and Spring Onion Salad

Serves 1

1 Little Gem lettuce, outer leaves removed
½ sun-dried tomato in oil, thoroughly drained
1–2 tomatoes, sliced
3–4 spring onions, chopped
3–4 walnut halves, chopped
Farmhouse Dressing (see page 80), to taste

1 Slice across the lettuce to give 6–7 round chunks and place in a bowl. Pat the sun-dried tomato dry on kitchen paper. Slice as thinly as possible and add to the bowl with the fresh tomatoes, spring onions and chopped walnut halves.

2 Add a little dressing. Toss the ingredients well and serve.

Fresh Sardine Salad and Citrus Mint Tabbouleh

Serves 1–2

1 lemon

300–350 ml (10–12 fl oz) Home-made
   Chicken or Vegetable Stock (see page 37)

50–75 g (2–3 oz) bulgar wheat

1–2 teaspoons olive oil

1 handful of mint, roughly chopped

2–3 medium/large fresh sardines, about
   50–75 g (2–3 oz) each

flat leaf parsley, to garnish

2 Bring the stock to the boil in a small pan. Add the bulgar wheat, reduce the heat and simmer, according to packet directions, until just cooked. Drain well, then add 1 teaspoon olive oil, the reserved lemon rind and juice and the fresh mint. Stir well and set aside – add a little more stock if the tabbouleh seems too dry.

3 Meanwhile, prepare the sardines. Scrape off the scales, remove and discard the heads, fins, tails and intestines. Rinse well under cold running water and pat dry with kitchen paper. Cook the sardines on a barbecue or under a preheated moderate grill and turn when they are sizzling – brush them with a very little olive oil or lemon juice, if liked, but they normally have sufficient oil to cook without this.

4 When the sardines are cooked through, serve them on top of the tabbouleh accompanied by the wedges of lemon and garnished with flat leaf parsley.

Viva Tomatoes on Toast

Serves 1

1 slice of sourdough bread
low-fat butter replacement, to spread
1 handful of cherry vine tomatoes, halved, or
    1 large vine tomato, sliced
1 tablespoon snipped chives
dash of Worcestershire sauce

1 Toast the slice of sourdough bread on both sides, then spread with the low-fat butter replacement.

2 Place the tomatoes on top of the toast and place under a preheated grill for a few minutes until soft.

3 Sprinkle the tomatoes with snipped chives and a little Worcestershire sauce and serve.

Chicory, Orange and Black Olive Salad

Serves 1

1 head of chicory, outer leaves removed
1 small orange, peeled
4–5 black olives
dash of balsamic vinegar

1 Divide the chicory into leaves and place in a bowl. Slice the orange and add the flesh and the juice to the chicory.

2 Add the olives and a dash of balsamic vinegar. Toss together well and serve.

variation

You can substitute radicchio for the chicory leaves in this salad for a colourful variation.

Artichoke, Endive and Green Herb Salad

Serves 1

2–3 artichoke hearts in oil, drained
5–6 endive leaves, torn
1 handful of herbs (such as basil, tarragon, parsley, chervil), chopped
Farmhouse Dressing (see page 80), to taste

1 Combine the vegetables and herbs in a bowl. Add the dressing to taste, toss well and serve.

Satsuma and Watercress Salad

Serves 2

2 handfuls of watercress
4 satsumas, peeled and segmented
4 pickled walnuts, halved or cut into wedges

1 Mix together the watercress and satsuma segments in a bowl. Add the pickled walnuts and serve.

variation

Combine 2 handfuls of watercress with the segments of 2 oranges and a few fresh mint leaves for slightly different fresh flavours.

Radish Rocket Salad

Try either of these two versions of a fiery fat-burning salad, which goes particularly well with chicken and egg dishes.

Serves 2

2 large handfuls of rocket

6–8 Cos lettuce leaves, sliced

10–15 cm (4–6 inch) piece of mooli, finely sliced, or

   12–16 radishes, halved

Dressing:

4 tablespoons balsamic vinegar

2 teaspoons clear honey

1 Place the rocket, lettuce leaves and mooli or radishes in a salad bowl.

2 Thoroughly combine the balsamic vinegar and honey and pour over the salad ingredients. Toss together well to coat and serve.

variation

Combine 2 large handfuls of watercress with 2 large handfuls of rocket and 12–16 small, halved radishes. Dress the salad with 4 tablespoons of freshly squeezed orange juice thoroughly mixed with 2 teaspoons of clear honey.

Warm Bean Salad with Fresh Herbs

Make this for a lunch at home or pack it in a box or flask – warm or chilled – to take for a packed lunch or picnic.

Serves 1–2

125 g (4 oz) okra, thickly sliced
1 large garlic clove, crushed
5–6 tablespoons water
3–4 tablespoons canned butter beans, drained and rinsed
3–4 tablespoons canned red kidney beans, drained and rinsed
1 teaspoon lemon or lime juice
1 teaspoon olive oil
1 small handful of fresh herbs (such as parsley, tarragon, chervil, coriander and dill or fennel), chopped
black pepper
1 thick slice of crusty wholemeal bread, to serve

1 Place the okra, garlic and water in a small saucepan. Cover and heat until boiling, then simmer gently for 3–4 minutes until soft. Drain.

2 Meanwhile, heat the butter beans and red kidney beans with the lemon or lime juice over a gentle heat. Strain, then add the okra and garlic with the olive oil, herbs and a little black pepper.

3 Stir gently and serve with a thick slice of crusty wholemeal bread, which you can use to mop up the delicious juices.

variation

You could substitute canned cannellini beans for the butter beans and borlotti beans for the kidney beans.

Green Bean and Egg Salad

You need fine, fresh green beans for this, topped and tailed, and roughly chopped. Alternatively, you can use sugar snap peas, mangetouts or sprue, very fine asparagus which is just as delicious but often less expensive.

Serves 2

250 g (8 oz) green beans, roughly chopped
6–8 cherry tomatoes, halved
2 garlic cloves, finely chopped
2 dessertspoons toasted pine nuts
2 teaspoons olive oil
4 tablespoons balsamic vinegar
2 eggs, hard-boiled and chopped
black pepper
2 slices of corn bread, to serve

1 Cook the beans (or other vegetables) briskly in a saucepan of boiling water for 5–10 minutes, until tender.

2 Drain the vegetables well, then return to the saucepan and add the halved cherry tomatoes, garlic, a little black pepper, the pine nuts, olive oil and balsamic vinegar. Stir gently to combine, add the chopped hard-boiled egg and stir gently again.

3 Serve warm with corn bread.

tip

To toast pine nuts, which brings out their flavour, spread them on a baking sheet and place in a hot oven or under a preheated grill for a few minutes. Keep checking and shaking the baking sheet so that they cook evenly. Watch the pine nuts carefully as they are quick to burn and will then taste bitter.

Smoked Trout and Rainbow Salad

This simple lunch comprises strips of smoked trout on a slice of fresh wholemeal barley bread, with a little Rainbow Salad.

Serves 1

1 slice of wholemeal barley bread
75–125 g (3–4 oz) smoked trout
Rainbow Salad:
1 handful of cress or torn green leaves (such as watercress, lettuce, rocket)
1 tomato, chopped
1–2 slices of cooked beetroot
1 heaped tablespoon grated carrot, turnip or parsnip, or sprouted seeds or grains
a few strips of yellow, green and/or red pepper
6–7 radishes
Farmhouse Dressing:
2 tablespoons cider vinegar or unsweetened apple juice
1 teaspoon clear honey or honeycomb
1 dessertspoon chopped mixed herbs (such as parsley, tarragon, chervil, fennel, dill)
salt and pepper

1 Put all the salad ingredients in a bowl and thoroughly mix together .

2 To make the dressing, place all the ingredients in a screw-top jar, season with salt and pepper and shake well to mix. Pour the dressing over the salad and toss well so that the leaves are coated in the dressing.

3 Arrange the dressed salad on the bread. Arrange the strips of trout on top and serve.

Slimmers' Coleslaw

This deliciously juicy coleslaw is packed with antioxidant vitamins and minerals and, unlike most 'dressed' coleslaws, is high in taste while low in calories. Sprouted onion seeds can be bought from well-stocked supermarkets.

Serves 1

¼ small cabbage
1–2 carrots
2 dessertspoons sprouted onion seeds or chopped chives
1 tablespoon raisins
1–2 tablespoons balsamic vinegar

1 Finely grate the cabbage and carrots into a large bowl. Add the sprouted onion seeds and raisins.

2 Add the balsamic vinegar and toss the coleslaw well to mix.

Stuffed Tomatoes

Serves 1

2 large tomatoes
½ small red onion, chopped
1 teaspoon olive oil
2 teaspoons lightly toasted pine nuts (see page 79)
¼ teaspoon ground allspice
1 tablespoon raisins
2–3 tablespoons boiled brown rice
salt and cayenne pepper
low-fat fromage frais, to serve

1 Slice a lid off each of the tomatoes, scrape out most of the pulp leaving the tomato 'shells' intact. Soften the onion in the oil. Add the pine nuts and allspice and cook until the pine nuts are golden. Stir in the tomato pulp, raisins, rice, salt and cayenne. Pack gently back into the tomato shells and replace the lids.

2 Place the stuffed tomatoes in a small ovenproof dish and bake in a preheated oven, 190°C (375°F), Gas 5, for 15–20 minutes until bubbling and tender.

3 Serve very hot with a little chilled fromage frais, dusted with cayenne pepper, spooned over.

Crab Salad

Buy some freshly prepared crab meat from your local fishmonger, or get him to dress whole crabs for you if you are entertaining and serve the meat in the shell. Alternatively, you could buy canned crab meat. Make sure you get some of the dark meat – its robust flavour perfectly offsets the blander, more delicate flavour of the white meat from the claws.

Serves 2

2 tablespoons alfalfa sprouts
2 handfuls of watercress
2 handfuls of lettuce, coarsely chopped
2 tomatoes, quartered
10 cm (4 inch) piece of cucumber, left unpeeled and chopped
6–8 red, green and/or yellow pepper strips
4–5 spring onions, chopped
175–250 g (6–8 oz) crab meat
Dressing:
2 tablespoons white wine vinegar
1 teaspoon demerara sugar
2 tablespoons chopped mint

1 Assemble the salad, placing the green leaves (alfalfa, watercress, lettuce), tomato, cucumber, pepper strips and spring onions in a large bowl.

2 To make the dressing, place the vinegar, sugar and mint in a screw-top jar, close and shake well to mix. Pour the dressing over the salad. Toss together well so that the vegetables are coated in the dressing. Arrange the salad on two plates.

3 Make sure the plates are absolutely dry of any surplus water from the salad vegetables, then place a portion of crab meat on each plate to serve.

Truffle Eggs

These are wonderful served for brunch or as a dinner party starter. You need a piece of truffle about the size of an index fingernail per person. Alternatives to the truffle are caviar or, less expensive but delicious, red or black lumpfish roe, smoked cod's roe, finely chopped anchovy fillets, smoked salmon, black olives or fresh chives.

Serves 2

2 eggs
2 small pieces of raw truffle, shaved
2 slices of bread, cut into thin narrow strips

1 Lightly soft-boil the eggs for about 3 minutes – cooked whites with runny yolks are essential for this recipe.

2 Allow the eggs to cool before handling, then cut a 'hat' off the pointed end of each one with a serrated knife. Carefully scrape out all the cooked egg into a bowl. Wash the empty shells and 'hats', flicking off any loose fragments. Wipe dry and set aside. Mix the little pieces of raw truffle with the egg and refill the shells.

3 Serve the eggs with thin narrow strips of your chosen bread, for dipping into the egg mixture.

Wilted Spinach with Eggs and Herb Butter

Serves 1

250–300 g (8–10 oz) fresh baby spinach, chopped
1 tablespoon water
2 eggs
15 g (½ oz) butter
1 teaspoon lemon juice
1 tablespoon chopped herbs (such as chives, chervil, tarragon, dill)
salt and pepper

1 Put the spinach in a saucepan with the water. Cover and cook over a medium heat for 1–2 minutes until just wilted. Keep warm.

2 Meanwhile, boil the eggs for about 3 minutes, according to your preference – the aim is to have set whites and runny yolks. Shell the eggs when they are cool enough to handle.

3 Heat the butter with the lemon juice. Remove from the heat and stir in the herbs and a little salt and pepper. Arrange the shelled eggs on the spinach and pour over the herb butter.

variation

You could make this dish with quail's eggs, which are delicious when soft boiled. Use two quail's eggs for every hen's egg and boil for only 2 minutes. Quail's eggs are rather difficult to shell.

Courgette Stuffed Mushrooms

Serves 2

2 very large flat mushrooms

1 garlic clove, crushed

2 teaspoons hot horseradish sauce or finely
   grated fresh horseradish

2 teaspoons lemon juice

75 g (3 oz) walnuts, chopped

1 small courgette, grated

2 teaspoons chopped rosemary

½ small onion, finely chopped

2 teaspoons olive oil

salt and pepper

chervil sprigs, to garnish

salad leaves, to serve

1 Remove and discard the mushroom stalks and place the caps, gill side uppermost, in a shallow ovenproof dish. Combine the garlic, horseradish and lemon juice in a small bowl and season to taste. Spread the mixture over the mushrooms.

2 Combine the walnuts, courgette, rosemary, onion and salt and pepper and spoon the mixture over the mushrooms, packing it down gently.

3 Drizzle the olive oil over the top and bake in a preheated oven, 190°C (375°F), Gas Mark 5, for 25–30 minutes until golden. Serve hot with salad leaves, garnished with chervil.

Bean Sprouts with Soy and Ginger

This is delicious and satisfying, and quick enough to prepare in a very brief lunch hour.

Serves 1

250 g (8 oz) bean sprouts
50–75 g (2–3 oz) canned bamboo shoots or water chestnuts, drained and thinly sliced
low-sodium soy sauce
½–1 cm (¼–½ inch) piece of fresh root ginger, finely chopped
1 tablespoon unsalted peanuts or cashew nuts

1 Immerse the bean sprouts in a saucepan of boiling water and return to the boil for 30 seconds until just softened. Add the bamboo shoots or water chestnuts and cook for a few seconds to heat through.

2 Strain very well, return to the pan and add the soy sauce, ginger and nuts. Transfer to a serving bowl.

Herb Omelette

Don't worry too much about the technique – untidy-looking omelettes taste just as nice as neat ones; the important thing is not to burn them.

Serves 1

1 teaspoon low-fat butter replacement
2 medium/large eggs
1 tablespoon cold water
2 tablespoons chopped herbs (such as chives, parsley, tarragon)
salt and pepper

1 Heat the fat in a nonstick frying pan or omelette pan over a medium heat.

2 Meanwhile, break the eggs into a clean dry bowl, add the water and salt and pepper and whisk in the herbs with a fork or balloon whisk until the mixture is pale and frothy.

3 When the fat sizzles, pour in the egg mixture and tip the pan so that the egg is spread evenly over the base. As the egg starts to cook around the edges of the pan, scrape the edges of the omelette towards the centre with a spatula to allow the uncooked egg to run underneath.

4 When the omelette looks set, give the pan a good shake to ensure it has not stuck – if it has, run the spatula gently underneath. Fold the omelette over, ease it out of the pan on to a warm plate and serve.

Fat-burner Steak Diane

Choose a fresh steak, as large as you like, and make sure it is trimmed of all visible fat.

Serves 1

1 rump or fillet steak, trimmed of fat
juice of 1 lime or ½ lemon
dash of Worcestershire sauce
2 teaspoons brandy
salt

1 Heat a nonstick frying pan until very hot and dry-fry the steak until cooked to your taste. As a very rough guide, cook a 3.5 cm (1½ inch) thick steak for 1½ minutes each side for rare, 2½–3 minutes each side for medium, and 3½–4 minutes each side for well done. You will need to reduce the heat slightly for the longer cooking times to avoid burning.

2 Remove the steak to a heated plate and keep warm while you deglaze the pan. Pour in the lime or lemon juice and a good dash of Worcestershire sauce and stir well, scraping any sediment from the base of the pan.

3 Remove from the heat, stir in the brandy, season with a little salt and pour the juices over the steak to serve.

tip

Fillet is the leanest cut of steak and also the most expensive. Rump tends to be lightly marbled with fat and is less tender than fillet, although many people consider it the best for frying.

Garlic Steak with Spring Vegetables

Serves 2

2–4 mint sprigs
2–4 new potatoes
1 bunch of young carrots (15–20)
2–4 tablespoons fresh garden peas
2 teaspoons olive oil
250–375 g (8–12 oz) top-quality organic
    steak, trimmed of fat
2 garlic cloves, thinly sliced
salt

1 Cook the potatoes in a large saucepan of lightly salted boiling water with the mint sprigs for about 10 minutes until almost tender. Add the carrots and cook for about 5 minutes until tender. Add the peas and cook for 2 minutes. Drain and keep warm.

2 Brush the oil over a frying pan and heat the pan. Meanwhile, make small cuts in the surface of the steak in several places and insert slivers of garlic.

3 When the pan is hot, add the steak and cook according to taste. As a very rough guide, cook a 3.5 cm (1½ inch) thick steak for 1½ minutes each side for rare, 2½–3 minutes each side for medium, and 3½–4 minutes each side for well done. You will need to reduce the heat slightly for the longer cooking times to avoid burning. Serve the steak with the tender spring vegetables.

Veal Schnitzel with Spinach and Brazil Nuts

Serves 2

2 tablespoons fresh wholemeal breadcrumbs
2 dessertspoons finely chopped Brazil nuts
2 tablespoons chopped thyme or 1 teaspoon
    dried thyme
1 egg, beaten
2 veal steaks, about 175 g (6 oz) each
2 teaspoons olive oil
200–400 g (7–13 oz) fresh baby spinach
1 tablespoon water
salt and pepper

1 Mix together the breadcrumbs, nuts, herbs and a little salt and pepper.

2 Break the egg into a clean bowl and beat well. Dip the veal steaks into the egg and then into the breadcrumb mixture, to coat.

3 Heat the oil in a nonstick frying pan, add the crumbed veal and gently fry over a medium heat for about 5–6 minutes on each side.

4 Meanwhile, cook the spinach in a large saucepan with the water until just wilted. Transfer to serving plates and arrange the veal on top.

Herb-Crusted Lamb with Spring Greens

Serves 4

finely grated rind of 1 lemon
1 tablespoon ground almonds
2–3 rosemary sprigs, finely chopped
1 tablespoon finely chopped flat leaf parsley
2 garlic cloves, chopped
2 pieces best end of neck of lamb, 4 or 5 cutlets on each rack
400 g (13 oz) spring greens
2 tablespoons lemon juice
salt and pepper

1 Combine the lemon rind, almonds, rosemary, parsley, garlic and a little salt and pepper.

2 Wipe the lamb with a damp cloth. Remove the fat, leaving just enough to prevent the meat from drying out. Place the meat in a roasting tin and spread the skinned side with the herb mixture, pressing it on well. Roast in a preheated oven, 200°C (400°F), Gas Mark 6, for 25 minutes.

3 Test whether the lamb is ready by sticking a skewer into the meat – the juices should run clear (unless you prefer your lamb pink, in which case reduce the cooking time slightly). When cooked, transfer the meat to a warmed plate for a short while before carving into cutlets.

4 Meanwhile, discard the outer leaves of the spring greens and shred the rest finely. Plunge into a large saucepan of boiling water and cook for 1–2 minutes until just tender.

5 Drain well and tip into the roasting tin to absorb the roasting juices. Season lightly. Stir in the lemon juice and serve with the roast lamb.

Mixed Grill

Serves 1

2 tiny lamb cutlets or 1 small lamb chop,
 trimmed of fat
1 slice of lamb's liver, rinsed and dried
2 lamb's kidneys, skinned and cored
2 tomatoes, halved
1 large field mushroom
lemon or lime juice, for brushing

1 Using a pastry brush, thoroughly moisten all the ingredients with lemon or lime juice.

2 Place them under a preheated medium grill and cook the lamb chop for 7–10 minutes each side (cutlets slightly less), and the liver and kidneys for 2–3 minutes each side, turning as required. Grill the tomatoes and mushroom for about 5 minutes, on one side only. Transfer to a plate and serve with the chop, liver and kidneys.

Chicken and Winter Vegetables

Serves 4

1–1.5 kg (2–3 lb) chicken
6–8 cloves
1 large onion, cut into wedges
2–3 carrots, chopped
¼ swede, cut into chunks
2–3 parsnips, cut into chunks
2–3 small turnips, cut into chunks
½ teaspoon dried mixed herbs
2–3 bay leaves
salt and pepper

1 Wipe the chicken inside and out with a damp cloth.

2 Bruise the heads of the cloves and stick them into the onion wedges by their stalks. Put the onion wedges in a large saucepan with a few pieces of carrot, then place the chicken on top. Fit all the other vegetable chunks under and around the chicken, season well with salt and pepper, add the herbs and enough water to just cover.

3 Bring to the boil quickly, skim off the scum that rises to the surface, then lower the heat, partially cover the pan and simmer slowly for 2½–3 hours, until the meat is very tender. You may need to top up the water.

4 Divide the chicken and vegetables among 4 plates and serve.

Harissa Chicken with Peppers

This is a quick, attractive and delicious main course for the family or guests. Buying peppers preserved in oil eliminates all that grilling and peeling preparation required for raw ones.

Serves 2

2 baking potatoes
1 teaspoon harissa paste
1 tablespoon water
2 chicken breasts, about 175 g (6 oz) each
2 garlic cloves, finely sliced
6–8 strips of red (or green) pepper preserved in oil, rinsed
  and dried
salt and pepper
1 tablespoon roughly chopped coriander,
  to garnish (optional)
leafy green salad, to serve

1 Thinly slice the potatoes and cook in boiling water for 6–8 minutes until almost tender. Drain and scatter in a small roasting tin. Mix the harissa paste with the water and use to coat the potatoes.

2 Using a sharp knife, cut small slits in the chicken breasts to aid even cooking, and pop a slice of garlic into each one. Place on the potatoes and lay the pepper strips on top of the chicken, together with any little bits of garlic left over. Season lightly with salt and pepper.

3 Bake in a preheated oven, 190°C (375°F), Gas Mark 5, until the chicken is cooked through. Scatter with coriander, if using, and serve with a leafy salad.

Italian Chicken with Pan-Fried Vegetables

Serves 4

300 g (10 oz) dried wholewheat pasta (such as tubes, bows, shells)

1 teaspoon olive oil

4 chicken breasts, about 175 g (6 oz) each, sliced into bite-size pieces

2–3 courgettes, sliced

125 g (4 oz) baby corn cobs, halved

12 black olives, drained

1 large beefsteak tomato, thickly sliced

1 tablespoon chopped parsley

1 tablespoon chopped mint

75 g (3 oz) low-fat cottage cheese

2 tablespoons balsamic vinegar

1 Cook the pasta in a large saucepan of boiling water for 10–15 minutes, or according to packet instructions until al dente – soft, but with a little bite.

2 Meanwhile, heat the oil in a large, heavy-based frying pan or sauté pan. Add the chicken and cook for 3–4 minutes. Add the courgettes and baby corn cobs and cook, covered, over a gentle heat for 7–10 minutes until tender.

3 Add the olives and slices of tomato, and cook for a further 4–5 minutes.

4 Drain the pasta when cooked and return to the pan. Add the cooked vegetables and chicken, the herbs and then the cottage cheese. Stir gently.

5 Arrange the pasta and chicken on 4 plates. Drizzle with the balsamic vinegar and serve.

Spiced Turkey on a Bed of Potato

Turkey breast provides excellent protein for increasing fat meltdown, and is rich in the amino acid tryptophan. This in turn increases serotonin levels, known to help chase away the blues and possibly to help with fat burning.

Serves 1

1 potato, peeled and cut into chunks

1 teaspoon wholegrain mustard

1 teaspoon ground paprika

1 teaspoon cumin seeds

1 teaspoon lime juice

1 tablespoon water

175–250 g (6–8 oz) turkey breast, thinly sliced

1 Cook the potato in boiling water until tender and cooked through.

2 Meanwhile, combine the mustard, paprika, cumin, lime juice and water. Pour the mixture over the turkey in a small pan and cook gently for about 15 minutes until the meat is tender and cooked through.

3 Drain the potato then sieve it on to a warmed plate. Top with the turkey and its cooking juices.

Prawns in Brandy Cream Sauce

Brandy is traditional for this recipe, but whisky works just as well.

Serves 2

2 tomatoes
2 teaspoons olive oil
2 spring onions, chopped
10–12 cooked peeled tiger prawns
2 tablespoons fresh or frozen peas
2 teaspoons capers, rinsed
2 tablespoons low-fat crème fraîche
2 dessertspoons brandy
black pepper
chervil sprigs, to garnish
4–6 tablespoons boiled brown rice, to serve

1 Place the tomatoes in a bowl and pour over boiling water to cover. Leave for 1–2 minutes, then drain, cut a cross at the stem end of each tomato and peel off the skins. Chop the flesh and set aside.

2 Heat the oil in a frying pan, add the spring onions and prawns and cook for 3 minutes. Add the tomatoes, peas and capers and stir in the crème fraîche with a good grinding of black pepper and the brandy. Stir to mix thoroughly and serve immediately on a bed of warm brown rice, garnished with chervil.

tip

You can make this dish almost as quickly with raw tiger prawns. Simply cook them until they turn pink. Always defrost frozen prawns thoroughly before use.

Salmon with Lemon, Parsley and Tarragon

Serves 2

2 thick salmon steaks, about 175 g (6 oz) each
grated rind and juice of 1 lemon
2 teaspoons olive oil
2 tablespoons chopped parsley
2 tablespoons chopped tarragon
black pepper

1 Brush the salmon on both sides with a little lemon juice and cook gently under a preheated medium grill for 3–4 minutes each side until cooked through.

2 Meanwhile, heat the olive oil with the remaining lemon juice and rind, then add the chopped herbs and the cooking juices from the grill pan. Season with pepper. Mix thoroughly and serve the salmon drizzled with the herby lemon oil mixture.

Pasta with Smoked Salmon and Asparagus

Serves 2

125–175 g (4–6 oz) dried wholewheat
spaghetti or other pasta
150 g (5 oz) asparagus tips
175 g (6 oz) smoked salmon, cut into pieces
4 heaped tablespoons low-fat fromage frais or
crème fraîche
2 tablespoons chopped tarragon, dill or parsley
freshly grated nutmeg, to taste

1 Cook the pasta in a large saucepan of boiling water until tender. Drain and return to the pan. Meanwhile, cook the asparagus tips in a frying pan containing 1 cm (½ inch) boiling water for 2 minutes until just tender. Drain.

2 Add the smoked salmon, fromage frais or crème fraîche, asparagus tips, chopped herbs and a little grated nutmeg to taste to the pasta. Mix thoroughly before serving.

93

Sautéed Monkfish with Green Gem Salad

Peeling the shelled broad beans to reveal the inner 'green gems' is slightly laborious, but well worth the effort. You can use canned or frozen broad beans instead of fresh, or substitute fresh or frozen garden peas if you prefer, although the flavour isn't the same.

Serves 2

125–250 g (4–8 oz) shelled broad beans
2 teaspoons olive oil
6–8 spring onions, chopped
250–375 g (8–12 oz) monkfish, cut into
    large chunks
2–4 dill or basil sprigs, roughly chopped
1 Little Gem lettuce or the inner leaves of
    ½ Cos lettuce, coarsely chopped
2 handfuls of watercress or alfalfa sprouts
½ green pepper, cored, deseeded and
    sliced lengthways
4–6 slices of cucumber, unpeeled
6–8 tablespoons Farmhouse Dressing (see
    page 80)

1 Cook the broad beans in a large saucepan of boiling water for about 5 minutes until tender. Drain, reserving the cooking liquid, and set aside to cool.

2 Meanwhile, heat the olive oil in a frying pan, add the spring onions and cook until softened.

3 Add the monkfish to the pan and turn to coat all over with the oil. Add the basil or dill, then cover and cook over a very low heat until the fish turns opaque and flakes easily.

4 Combine the lettuce, watercress or alfalfa, green pepper and cucumber in a bowl. Dress with a little Farmhouse Dressing and keep the salad cool while you peel the beans.

5 When the beans are cool enough to handle, nick the rather tough outer skin of each bean with the tip of a sharp knife, widen slightly, press gently and the bright green, velvety bean will pop out. Add the beans to the salad and arrange on a plate. Gently place the monkfish and spring onions on top, pour over any pan juices and serve.

Seafood Vermicelli with Tomato and Mushroom Sauce

This is a quick and delicious meal, but don't even think of using shellfish bottled in vinegar or brine. Use frozen shelled cockles and mussels if fresh ones are unavailable and allow them to defrost before using.

Serves 3–4

250 g (8 oz) fresh egg or dried wholewheat vermicelli
2 teaspoons olive oil
1 onion, finely sliced
1 garlic clove, crushed or finely chopped
175 g (6 oz) oyster mushrooms, torn into large pieces
5–6 large tomatoes, chopped or 400 g (13 oz) can tomatoes, roughly chopped
125 g (4 oz) freshly cooked shelled cockles
125 g (4 oz) freshly cooked shelled mussels
1 dessertspoon snipped chives
salt and pepper
basil sprigs, to garnish

1 Cook the vermicelli in a large saucepan of boiling water for about 10 minutes or according to packet instructions until al dente – soft, but with a little bite.

2 Meanwhile, heat the olive oil in a medium saucepan. Add the onion and garlic and cook over a low heat, stirring occasionally, until softened. Add the mushrooms and tomatoes – with their juice if using canned or with a little boiling water if using fresh – together with the cockles and mussels.

3 Cook for 5–7 minutes over a medium heat, stirring, until cooked through. Add the chives. Stir well and season to taste with salt and pepper.

4 Drain the vermicelli when cooked and arrange on individual plates. Pour the seafood sauce over the top and garnish with basil sprigs.

Whiting Stoker with Green Beans and Cayenne Potato

Buy the freshest fish you can find – any flat white fish can be used, but this method brings out the delicate flavour of whiting very well.

Serves 1

1 whiting fillet, about 175–200 g (6–7 oz)
3–4 tablespoons water
75–125 g (3–4 oz) green beans
2 teaspoons olive oil
lime juice, to taste
1 tablespoon flaked almonds
Cayenne Potato:
1 baking potato
a little skimmed milk, to mix
2–3 spring onions, chopped
pinch of cayenne pepper
low-fat butter replacement or fromage frais,
   to serve

1 To make the cayenne potato, wash the potato, pat it dry and score all the way around the middle with a sharp knife. Bake in a preheated oven, 230°C (450°F), Gas Mark 8, for 1 hour or until tender.

2 When the potato is cooked, cut around the score mark and separate the two halves. Scoop out the potato flesh into a bowl and mash with just enough skimmed milk to achieve the consistency you like. Mix in the chopped spring onions and cayenne pepper to taste and pile back into the shells.

3 Place the fish on a large heatproof plate suitable for steaming or for use in a microwave. Pour over the water and cover. To steam the fish, set the plate over a saucepan of boiling water. Cover and steam gently for 6–8 minutes or until cooked. To microwave the fish, cover it and cook on medium power for 2–4 minutes depending on your oven and the thickness of the fish. Check the fish halfway through – it is cooked when the flesh is opaque and flakes easily.

4 Meanwhile, cook the green beans in a saucepan of boiling water for a few minutes until al dente, and place the potato halves under a preheated grill to brown. Drain the beans and mix with the olive oil, lime juice and flaked almonds.

5 Serve the fish with the green beans and potatoes. Eat the beautifully crisp potato skins, spread with some of the low-fat butter replacement or some very cold low-fat fromage frais from your daily allowance and a little more cayenne pepper, if liked.

Vegetarian Sausages with Tomato and Herb Mash

Serves 1

1 large or 2 medium potatoes, peeled and cut
 into chunks

1 teaspoon olive oil

2–3 vegetarian or Quorn sausages

2 tomatoes, thinly sliced

1 large garlic clove, crushed

½ onion, thinly sliced into rings (optional)

dash of Worcestershire or Tabasco sauce

2 teaspoons finely chopped thyme

3–4 tablespoons skimmed milk

black pepper

basil sprigs, to garnish

1 Cook the potato chunks in saucepan of boiling water for 20 minutes until soft.

2 Meanwhile, heat the olive oil in a shallow pan and gently cook the sausages. Remove from the pan and keep warm.

3 Place the tomato slices in the hot pan with the garlic and onions, if using, and cook over a medium heat, turning frequently, for 4–5 minutes until soft. Season with a dash of Worcestershire sauce or Tabasco.

4 Drain the potatoes well, then mash with the thyme and milk and season with black pepper.

5 Remove the skins from the cooked tomatoes, then mix the tomatoes and onions, if using, with the mashed potato. Season with a little black pepper and place on a warmed plate with the sausages arranged on top. Garnish with basil sprigs and serve.

variation

You can flavour the mash with a variety of herbs and spices, including garlic, parsley, chives or saffron.

Tomato and Courgette Bake

Serves 2

200 g (7 oz) small vine tomatoes, halved
2 small courgettes, thinly sliced
2 teaspoons chopped thyme
2 garlic cloves, finely chopped
2 teaspoons olive oil
4 eggs
3 tablespoons semi-skimmed milk
2 tablespoons freshly grated Parmesan cheese
salt and pepper
salad leaves, to serve

1 Lightly oil a 900 ml (1½ pint) shallow ovenproof dish or two individual dishes and scatter with the tomatoes, courgettes, thyme and garlic. Season lightly with salt and pepper. Add the oil and toss to mix. Bake in a preheated oven, 200°C (400°F), Gas Mark 6, for 10 minutes.

2 Lightly beat the eggs with the milk and a little salt and pepper and pour the mixture over the vegetables. Sprinkle with the cheese and bake for a further 30 minutes until golden and lightly set. Serve with salad leaves.

Steamed Vegetables with Guacamole Topping

Serves 1

2–3 carrots, sliced lengthways
1 handful of broccoli florets
1 handful of cauliflower florets
½ large or 1 medium leek, sliced into rings
125 g (4 oz) fresh green beans
½ avocado, mashed
1 spring onion, finely chopped
1 teaspoon curry paste
1 teaspoon chopped coriander
2 cherry tomatoes, chopped
garlic salt and pepper

1 Place the carrots, broccoli, cauliflower, leek and green beans in a metal steamer or sieve and set it over a saucepan of boiling water for 10–12 minutes until the vegetables are crisp to the bite but not too soft. Alternatively, cook the vegetables in an electric steamer.

2 Meanwhile, spoon the avocado flesh into a bowl and mix with the spring onion, curry paste, coriander, tomatoes and a little garlic salt and pepper, using a fork.

3 Drain the vegetables when cooked and arrange on a plate. Top with the guacamole and serve.

Sautéed Artichokes with Brazil Nuts

Substitute a little vegetable broth if you do not have a juicer to make fresh carrot juice.

Serves 2

1 onion, thinly sliced
1 teaspoon olive oil
8–10 canned artichoke hearts in brine, rinsed and halved
300 ml (½ pint) freshly prepared carrot juice
grated rind and juice of 1 lime
175 g (6 oz) Brazil nuts, chopped
1 tablespoon snipped chives
pinch of freshly grated nutmeg
salt and pepper
steamed green vegetables, to serve

1 Gently fry the onion in the olive oil in a frying pan until soft but not brown.

2 Add the halved artichoke hearts and carrot juice. Stir in the lime rind and juice, Brazil nuts, chives, nutmeg and salt and pepper until well blended and piping hot. Serve immediately with green vegetables.

Flageolet and Mushroom Savoury

Serves 2

200 g (7 oz) can flageolet beans or other pulses, drained and rinsed

100 ml (3½ fl oz) Vegetable Stock (see page 37)

1–2 garlic cloves, crushed

125–175 g (4–6 oz) field mushrooms, sliced

1 teaspoon low-fat butter replacement

1 tablespoon lemon juice

1 heaped tablespoon chopped parsley

25 g (1 oz) wholemeal breadcrumbs

25 g (1 oz) low-fat vegetarian cheese, grated

1 Put the beans and stock in a saucepan with the garlic. Heat until warmed through, then strain off most of the liquid into a pan containing the mushrooms. Cover the pan and cook the mushrooms for about 4–5 minutes, or until soft.

2 Meanwhile, place the beans and some of the remaining cooking liquid in a food processor or blender and purée to the consistency of single cream. Stir in the butter replacement, lemon juice, cooked mushrooms and parsley. Mix well and tip into a flameproof dish.

3 Top the mixture with the breadcrumbs and grated cheese and brown under a preheated hot grill for a few minutes before serving.

Strawberries with Crème Fraîche and Grand Marnier

Serves 1

125–175 g (4–6 oz) strawberries
1 teaspoon grated orange rind
1 tablespoon freshly squeezed orange juice,
   Cointreau or Grand Marnier
2 tablespoons low-fat crème fraîche, chilled

1 Rinse and hull the strawberries and dry on kitchen paper.

2 Mix together the remaining ingredients, spoon over the fruit and serve.

Minty Citrus Replete

Serves 1

½ large grapefruit, ugli fruit or pomelo
½ small orange or 1 mandarin
shredded mint or lemon balm, to taste
1 teaspoon clear honey or maple syrup
1–2 drops pure peppermint oil

1 Working over a bowl, carefully remove the segments of grapefruit, ugli fruit or pomelo from its skin and discard the seeds and pith. Reserve the grapefruit skin. Segment the orange or mandarin in the same way, again discarding the seeds and pith.

2 Mix the citrus segments with the shredded herbs, honey or maple syrup and peppermint oil. Pile back into the grapefruit skin and glaze for 30–60 seconds under a preheated hot grill before serving.

tip

Ugli fruit is a hybrid of the grapefruit, orange and tangerine. It is similar to grapefruit in flavour, but sweeter. The pomelo is a pear-shaped citrus fruit with a thick, green skin. It is similar to grapefruit in flavour, but not so juicy.

Fruit Fanfare

Serves 1

1 large slice of melon

1 small bunch of seedless grapes (about 15–20)

5–6 cherries, pitted

1 mandarin orange, segmented

3–4 mint sprigs, chopped

5 mm (¼ inch) piece of fresh root ginger, finely chopped

1 Chop the melon flesh and place in a small bowl. Add the remaining fruit, the mint leaves and the ginger. Mix well.

2 Chill thoroughly in the refrigerator before serving.

Walnut and Honey Yogurt

You should be able to buy honeycomb from a number of places, such as healthfood stores, delicatessens or farm shops selling local produce.

Serves 1

1 dessertspoon honeycomb

100–200 ml (3½–7 fl oz) low-fat, thick natural yogurt

6–7 walnut halves

1 Cut the honeycomb into pieces to release the liquid honey from the cells.

2 Stir the honey into the yogurt with the walnut halves and serve chilled.

Persimmon Cream

Persimmons are a full red/orange colour when ripe, and feel very soft when squeezed.

Serves 1

1 large persimmon
1 tablespoon low-fat crème fraîche

1 Slice the top off the fruit. Scoop out the fleshy contents into a small bowl and reserve the skin. Add the crème fraîche to the bowl and mix well.

2 Return the persimmon cream to the reserved skin, working carefully because the fleshy 'walls' of the ripe fruit are delicate and easily ruptured. Serve.

Traditional Baked Apple

This provides negative calories, plus lots of fibre and nutrients to satisfy hunger pangs and boost metabolism.

Serves 1

1 large dessert apple
2–3 cloves
2 tablespoons mixed raisins and sultanas
1 teaspoon clear honey
pinch of ground cinnamon
1 teaspoon brandy (optional)
low-fat natural yogurt, fromage frais or soya
    milk yogurt, to serve

1 Remove and discard the core of the apple using an apple corer. Score around the middle of the apple with a sharp knife to allow it to swell without bursting. Bruise the cloves and push them into the apple.

2 Place the apple in an ovenproof dish or small roasting tin. Mix together the dried fruit, honey and cinnamon and spoon the mixture into the hollowed centre of the apple. Add a teaspoon of brandy if liked. Pour a little hot water into the dish or roasting tin.

3 Cook in a preheated oven, 200°C (400°F), Gas Mark 6, for 45 minutes–1 hour, until very soft. After about 20 minutes baste the apple with the juices in the dish.

4 Serve hot, warm or chilled with a little low-fat natural yogurt, fromage frais or soya milk yogurt.

Grilled Pears with Oatmeal and Raspberry Cream

Serves 1

1 pear, halved
1 teaspoon unrefined icing sugar
2 teaspoons low-fat thick Greek yogurt
2 teaspoons medium oatmeal, toasted
2 dessertspoons raspberries
mint sprigs, to decorate

1 Scoop the cores from the pear halves and place the fruit in a flameproof dish. Dust with the icing sugar and cook under a preheated moderate grill for 3–4 minutes until beginning to colour.

2 Tip the yogurt into a small bowl. Fold in the oatmeal and raspberries, then spoon the mixture into the centres of the pear halves and serve decorated with mint sprigs and a few raspberries.

Warm Pineapple Gratin

Serves 2

4 thick slices of pineapple
2 teaspoons pineapple liqueur or brandy (optional)
½ teaspoon vanilla extract
4 tablespoons low-fat fromage frais, chilled
2 teaspoons light muscovado sugar

1 Place the slices of pineapple in a shallow flameproof dish and sprinkle with the pineapple liqueur or brandy, if using.

2 Stir the vanilla into the fromage frais and spoon the mixture over the pineapple. Sprinkle the sugar over the top, then place under a preheated grill for a few minutes until the sugar is bubbling. Serve at once.

Lychees with Almond Junket

Junket is an old English country dish and was part of staple fare long before the advent of yogurt. Rennet, available from health food stores, is produced from an enzyme found in a cow's stomach and is used for creating curds (milk solids) and whey (the watery part). Warming the milk above blood temperature (98.4°F/37°C) will inactivate the rennet and your junket will not set.

Serves 2–3

600 ml (1 pint) semi-skimmed milk

1 dessertspoon demerara sugar

1–2 teaspoons rennet

2–3 drops of real almond essence

250 g (8 oz) can lychees in juice or 250 g (8 oz) fresh
  lychees, skinned and poached in a little water

1 Gently heat the semi-skimmed milk in a pan to blood temperature. (When you dip your little finger into the milk, it registers neither hot nor cold.)

2 Pour the warmed milk into a dish and stir in the demerara sugar, rennet and almond essence. Cover and leave to set, then chill in the refrigerator.

3 When the junket is set, cut criss-crosses through it with a knife, and place the lychees between the resulting diamond-shaped curds, together with a little juice.

tip

Vegetarian rennet, derived from plant sources or manufactured synthetically, is also available.

Arabian Apricots

Select really soft, tender apricots for this recipe. Tahini is a thick, oily, light brown paste of crushed toasted sesame seeds. It often separates on standing in the jar, so stir it well before using.

Serves 1

6 presoaked dried apricots
3 teaspoons tahini
ground cinnamon, to taste
6 freshly blanched almonds
1 teaspoon unrefined icing sugar

1 Cut a slit in each apricot. Insert ½ teaspoon of tahini mixed with a pinch of ground cinnamon and one blanched almond into each apricot.

2 Reshape the apricots. Sprinkle with icing sugar and set aside for dessert.

Redcurrant Glass Ceiling

Here, demerara sugar is sprinkled over wet redcurrants and left overnight. The sugar and redcurrant juices mingle to form a delicious 'glassy' crust.

Serves 2

250–300 g (8–10 oz) redcurrants
2–4 dessertspoons demerara sugar
½ teaspoon ground cinnamon

1 Remove the redcurrants from their stalks and wash. Place in a dish while still wet.

2 Combine the demerara sugar with the ground cinnamon, then sprinkle the mixture over the redcurrants. Place the dish in the refrigerator and leave overnight.

Apple and Blueberry Crumble

Serves 2

2 crisp dessert apples
2 tablespoons water
small handful of blueberries
25 g (1 oz) porridge oats
2 teaspoons light olive oil
1 tablespoon light muscovado sugar
25 g (1 oz) sultanas or raisins
mint sprigs, to decorate
low-fat Greek yogurt, to serve

1 Peel, core and slice the apples. Put in a small pan with the water. Cover and cook gently until the apples have softened. Stir in three-quarters of the blueberries and remove from the heat. Allow to cool.

2 Meanwhile, put the oats, oil, sugar and dried fruit in a frying pan and cook, stirring constantly, until the oats are golden. Allow to cool.

3 Divide the apple mixture between two dessert glasses and spoon the oat mixture on top. Top with a spoonful of yogurt, the remaining blueberries and mint sprigs to decorate.

- ▶ Why other diets fail

- ▶ Two weeks on/two weeks off

- ▶ Boosting the fat-burning fires

- ▶ Coffee and tea

- ▶ Exercise

- ▶ Making your fat-burner foods work

6 Just to Remind You...

why other diets fail

Fad diets work (briefly) for a number of reasons, not the least being the 'short sharp shock' they deliver to your digestive, glandular, muscular and other systems. The body does react with weight loss when you feed it nothing but, say, lettuce, tomato and cottage cheese, or steak, grapes and spinach, after months or years of making poor food choices for weight control.

This weight loss does tend to comprise mainly water because such eating plans rely on the metabolic shock of an enormously reduced calorie intake without the help of fat-burner foods. It is also next to impossible to sustain such diets for any length of time, because sooner or later our taste buds will revolt at the fare they are being offered. Never – we feel – will we be able to look a carton of low-fat cottage cheese or a lettuce leaf in the face again. Boredom is the arch enemy of the serious weight-loser, and one you need never do battle with on the Fat-burner Foods Weight Loss Programme.

people in a hurry...

remember less than they think – and hope – they will. It is undoubtedly boring and tiring to read or hear the same old thing time and time again when you are so stressed and busy that you hardly have a moment to yourself to breathe freely.

But habits, especially unhealthy ones, become entrenched simply because we repeat them over and over again. It is important, therefore, to be reminded of the importance of alternating your two 14-day plans – the Fat-burner Foods Rapid Fat Loss Plan and the Fat-burner Foods Stabilizer Plan.

two weeks on/two weeks off

So, to remind you, here's what you have to do:

1 Follow the FBF Rapid Fat Loss Plan in Chapter 3 for exactly two weeks. (Week 2 is a repetition of Week 1.) Weigh yourself first thing every morning, without clothes, after going to the toilet. Record your weight on the charts provided on pages 122–123.

2 Follow this immediately – don't be tempted to have a complete rest for a few days – with two weeks on one of the four FBF Stabilizer Plans. (Again, Week 2 is a repetition of Week 1.)

3 If you have more fat to burn, back you go on the Rapid Fat Loss Plan.

4 After two weeks, come off the Rapid Fat Loss Plan again, and on to your choice of FBF Stabilizer Plans.

5 Continue in this way following the Programme exactly, that is two weeks on the Rapid Fat Loss Plan, followed by two weeks on your choice of Stabilizer Plan, as often as you need, until you reach 1–1.5 kg (2–3 lb) below your goal weight, or 0.5 kg (1 lb) if you had only a few pounds to lose to start off with.

6 Continue to check your weight daily or, at the very least, weekly. If your weight should ever climb to 0.5–1 kg (1–2 lb) above your target weight, go back on the FBF Weight Loss Programme until you return to your earlier desirable weight. It really is that simple.

boosting the fat-burning fires

To help yourself achieve your personal goal, continue to vary your diet as much as possible, utilizing the fullest possible range of fat-burner foods and tips. Never go hungry – there's no need – and never despair. Many of the people who have lost all the fat they wanted on the Fat-burner Foods Weight Loss Programme had been overweight for ten, twenty, and in some cases for over thirty years.

There are various ways you can boost your fat-burning fires on the Fat-burner Foods Weight Loss Programme, such as drinking plenty of water and eating breakfast. All these tips are just as useful after you have reached your target weight, when you are determined to remain slim, active and healthy. In addition, don't even think about missing meals or cutting back too drastically on fat – either way, your metabolism will feel threatened by starvation, and drop right down to protect you. Your calorie-burning power therefore tumbles.

Too much fat, on the other hand, may make you eat too much and cancel some of the fat-melting effects of your eating plan. Very overweight people tend to have their appetites stimulated by a high-fat meal, while lean people do not. It is thought that, probably owing to insulin resistance (see page 22), a high fat intake makes an overweight person hungry for more fat-laden foods.

One important part of the FBF Weight Loss Programme is 'grazing', which means eating frequent small meals and permitted snacks, including low-fat protein foods, such as cottage cheese, chicken and fish. Five to six hours during the day is too long to go empty. Three meals a day will raise the metabolic rate by up to 200 calories per 24 hours and grazing boosts it even higher.

A whole range of nutrients work together to produce energy, particularly B group vitamins. Good choices include whole grains, corn, fish and chicken because they can use up more energy than they supply – this means they are also sources of negative calories.

coffee and tea

Be healthwise about coffee and tea. Both tea and coffee increase the rate of metabolism. Enjoy as much as you want of either or both, unless they give you heartburn or palpitations, or you have a heart condition.

A study of green tea reported in the *European Journal of Clinical Nutrition* in 2000, tested the effects of drinking three different strengths – 2.5 g (⅛ oz) of dried leaves in 150 ml (¼ pint) of water, 5 g (¼ oz) in 300 ml (½ pint), and 7.5 g (⅓ oz) in 450 ml (¾ pint) – in 10 healthy adults. A standardized laboratory test was used to measure the capacity of the volunteers' plasma (the liquid part of the bloodstream) to neutralize free radicals, harmful molecular fragments that can cause premature ageing, heart disease and cancer. Blood samples were taken one and two hours after drinking the tea, and the two higher doses of tea were found to increase antioxidant activity by about 7 and 12 per cent respectively. This is very good news for general health and might indicate that other nutrients more directly concerned with energy production were equally active.

exercise

Exercise, too, as everyone is aware, revs up fat burning (see Chapter 7). According to Ian Marber, author of *The Food Doctor in the City*, it enhances the metabolic rate by multiplying the number of mitochondria in muscle cells (mitochondria are the microscopic power houses within cells which convert glucose into energy). Regular exercise sustained for 25–30 minutes four or five times a week can have a significant effect on fat-burning, raising energy consumption for up to 18 hours afterwards.

Making Your Fat-burner Foods Work

ACTION	EFFECT	TO HELP YOU...
Drink at least 8 glasses of water daily	Avoids dehydration, which reduces metabolic rate by 2–3 per cent. Vary the types of water, such as still mineral water, tap water and specialist spring waters.	Add a slice of lemon or lime, or drink hot water flavoured with a pinch of ground nutmeg or cinnamon or small pieces of chopped fresh root ginger.
Eat breakfast	Raises metabolic rate by between 10 and 25 per cent.	Divide your breakfast into two or three snacks if you really cannot eat shortly after waking, for example drink some fruit juice to start the day, eat low-fat yogurt when you get to work/college and an apple mid-morning.
Avoid crash-dieting	Lowers metabolic rate and deprives you of essential nutrients.	The nutritionally sound Rapid Fat Loss Plan is hard-hitting like some crash diets, but prevents the fall in metabolism that unwise diets can cause.
Spread your fat over the course of a day	When you are very overweight a lot of fat eaten all at once can sharpen the appetite for further fat.	Save the low-fat butter replacement intended for breakfast for your lunchtime bread, and eat low-fat yogurt or cheese in the later part of the day. Avoid cheese last thing if it makes you dream, although calcium-rich foods can calm the nerves and help promote sound sleep.
'Graze' instead of eating one or two heavy meals per day with long gaps between	'Grazing' uses up to 200 extra calories over 24 hours – just under 25 g (1 oz) fat per 24 hours.	Most meals can be divided into at least two parts. Eat little and often – every 2–3 hours.

114

ACTION	EFFECT	TO HELP YOU...
Eat negative calorie foods daily	They boost fat-burning by using up more calories than they supply.	Many vegetables and low-GI items are negative calorie foods (see page 27).
Drink tea and coffee (see page 113)	Increases metabolic rate and fat burning.	Avoid too many cups of strong, bitter Mediterranean- or Greek-style black coffee, especially on an empty stomach. It can cause nausea and vomiting.
Eat all the spicy foods you enjoy, often	Spices not only perk up bland foods, they also whizz up your metabolic rate by a hefty 25 per cent. Chilli pepper, cayenne and hot mustard should all hit the spot.	You can add all the spices you like to your Fat-burning Soup and to Stabilizer Plan recipes as well.
Exercise! **IMPORTANT: Consult your doctor before starting an exercise programme if you have a medical condition or any health concerns.**	Increases metabolic rate and fat-burning by multiplying the number of muscle mitochondria (cellular power houses converting glucose into energy). Regular exercise sustained for 25–30 minutes four or five times a week fans the fat-burning flames within, for up to 18 hours afterwards. Brisk walking, cycling, dancing and swimming are all safe forms of aerobic exercise (the type that makes you slightly out of breath). Simply becoming more active in your everyday routine is also very beneficial.	Drink a cup of coffee 1 hour before exercising. Caffeine triggers the release of fat into the blood, which the exercise will then burn. Iced coffee is delicious in hot weather or any time you fancy. Skimmed milk makes excellent cappuccino – just invest in a hand-held milk frother. Replace fattening chocolate powder with ground cinnamon or nutmeg sprinkled on your cappuccino instead – many coffee shops will do this if you ask.

115

▶ **Deep breathing**

▶ **Weight training**

▶ **Aerobic exercise, plus activity and
   energy use chart**

116

7　Lighting the Fire Within

deep breathing

Do deep breathing exercises on waking in the morning, before going to sleep at night and at least once during the day.

Stand easily – or lie down, if you happen to be in bed. Take a deep breath S-L-O-W-L-Y over a count of 5 seconds – use a watch or count 'one-thousand-two-thousand...' at medium speed to check the time. Fill your lungs as full as possible.

Hold your breath for 20 seconds, or for as long as you can without straining yourself, and then breathe out again very slowly to a count of 10. Repeat a total of 15 times.

You will see and feel your abdomen expanding in addition to your chest as you breathe in; you will also feel calmer and more stress free, as well as having increased energy.

weight training

Some authorities claim that this is the best fat-burning exercise on the grounds that the metabolism continues to burn at an increased rate for 24 hours after a 60-minute workout. Such a figure (and those of the exercise types in the chart above), can be misleading since we vary so much as individuals. However, weight training does have in its favour the development of greater lean

muscle mass with its ability to utilize surplus calories more much efficiently.

It also firms and tones the figure, while combating any muscular wastage that can result from prolonged dieting and, together with aerobic exercise or increased daily activity, helps to boost the body's metabolism when the calorie intake is reduced.

aerobic exercise

Aerobic exercise makes you slightly breathless and increases your pulse rate. There are plenty of books and videos on working out safely, but it is safest to check with your doctor before starting aerobic exercise for the first time, especially if you have any health concerns. To obtain maximum fat-burning benefits, you should aim eventually to exercise for about 30–40 minutes at a stretch, three to five times a week.

It's important to choose something you enjoy, be it horse riding, aqua-aerobics or jazz dance. Share your new activity with a friend, or join a class for mutual support and a good laugh!

Build your new activity gradually into your lifestyle. If you do it five days a week for a fortnight, the chances are that you will go right off it and never do it again. The box on this page gives a guide to some activities, together with the energy they use per hour.

Some of these activities – mowing the lawn, window cleaning and housework, are more work than pleasure. So by simply increasing your overall daily activity you can significantly improve overall fitness and energy levels – even if it has less fat-burning boost than the more demanding stuff. Simple ways to do this include using the stairs instead of lifts or escalators, parking further from your destination and walking the rest of the way, and getting up from your desk every hour for a walk around the office or home.

ACTIVITY AND ENERGY USE

Activity	Calories/hour
Bowling	250
Cleaning windows	350
Cycling	400
Dancing	300
Football	450
Gardening	250
General housework	190
Golf	250
Horse riding	450
Ironing	250
Jogging	500
Mowing the lawn	400
Running	900
Scrubbing floors	275
Skiing	500
Swimming	500
Walking	250

Desirable Weight Ranges

WOMEN

Height	1.45m	4 ft 9 in	1.65m	5 ft 5 in
Small frame	40.82 kg – 43.10 kg	90 lb – 97 lb	51.71 kg – 55.80 kg	114 lb –123 lb
Medium frame	42.64 kg – 48.08 kg	94 lb – 106 lb	54.43 kg – 61.24 kg	120 lb –135 lb
Large frame	46.27 kg – 53.52 kg	102 lb – 118 lb	58.51 kg – 66.23 kg	129 lb –146 lb
Height	1.47m	4 ft 10 in	1.68m	5 ft 6 in
Small frame	41.73 kg – 45.36 kg	92 lb –100 lb	53.52 kg – 57.61 kg	118 lb –127 lb
Medium frame	43.10 kg – 49.44 kg	97 lb –109 lb	56.25 kg – 63.05 kg	124 lb –139 lb
Large frame	47.63 kg – 54.89 kg	105 lb –121 lb	60.33 kg – 68.04 kg	133 lb –150 lb
Height	1.50m	4 ft 11 in	1.70m	5 ft 7 in
Small frame	43.09 kg – 46.72 kg	95 lb –103 lb	55.34 kg – 59.42 kg	122 lb –131 lb
Medium frame	45.36 kg – 50.80 kg	100 lb –112 lb	58.06 kg – 64.86 kg	128 lb –143 lb
Large frame	48.99 kg – 56.25 kg	108 lb –124 lb	62.14 kg – 69.85 kg	137 lb –154 lb
Height	1.52m	5 ft	1.72m	5 ft 8 in
Small frame	44.45 kg – 48.08 kg	98 lb –106 lb	57.15 kg – 61.69 kg	126 lb –136 lb
Medium frame	46.72 kg – 52.16 kg	103 lb –115 lb	59.88 kg – 66.68 kg	132 lb –147 lb
Large frame	50.35 kg – 57.61 kg	111 lb –127 lb	63.96 kg – 72.12 kg	141 lb –159 lb
Height	1.55m	5 ft 1 in	1.75m	5 ft 9 in
Small frame	45.81 kg – 49.44 kg	101 lb –109 lb	58.97 kg – 63.50 kg	130 lb –140 lb
Medium frame	48.08 kg – 53.53 kg	106 lb –118 lb	61.69 kg – 68.49 kg	136 lb –151 lb
Large frame	51.71 kg – 58.97 kg	114 lb –130 lb	65.77 kg – 74.39 kg	145 lb –164 lb
Height	1.57m	5 ft 2 in	1.78m	5 ft 10 in
Small frame	47.17 kg – 50.80 kg	104 lb –112 lb	60.33 kg – 65.32 kg	133 lb –144 lb
Medium frame	49.44 kg – 55.34 kg	109 lb –122 lb	58.97 kg – 70.31 kg	140 lb –155 lb
Large frame	53.07 kg – 60.78 kg	117 lb –134 lb	67.59 kg – 76.66 kg	149 lb –169 lb
Height	1.60m	5 ft 3 in	1.80m	5 ft 11 in
Small frame	48.53 kg – 52.16 kg	107 lb –115 lb	62.15 kg – 67.14 kg	137 lb –147 lb
Medium frame	50.80 kg – 57.15 kg	112 lb –126 lb	60.79 kg – 72.13 kg	147 lb –159 lb
Large frame	54.89 kg – 62.60 kg	121 lb –138 lb	69.41 kg – 78.48 kg	153 lb –173 lb
Height	1.63m	5 ft 4 in	1.83m	6 ft
Small frame	49.70 kg – 53.98 kg	110 lb –119 lb	63.97 kg – 68.96 kg	140 lb –150 lb
Medium frame	52.62 kg – 59.42 kg	116 lb –131 lb	62.61 kg – 73.95 kg	150 lb –162 lb
Large frame	56.70 kg – 64.41 kg	125 lb –142 lb	71.23 kg – 80.30 kg	156 lb –176 lb

Figures adapted from those provided by
the Metropolitan Life Insurance Company, New York, 1959.

MEN

Height	1.55m	5 ft 1 in	1.75m	5 ft 9 in
Small frame	47.63 kg – 51.26 kg	105 lb – 113 lb	60.33 kg – 64.87 kg	133 lb – 143 lb
Medium frame	50.35 kg – 55.34 kg	111 lb – 122 lb	63.05 kg – 69.40 kg	139 lb – 153 lb
Large frame	53.98 kg – 60.78 kg	119 lb – 134 lb	67.13 kg – 75.73 kg	148 lb – 167 lb

Height	1.57m	5 ft 2 in	1.78m	5 ft 10 in
Small frame	48.99 kg – 52.62 kg	108 lb –116 lb	62.14 kg – 66.68 kg	137 lb – 147 lb
Medium frame	51.71 kg – 57.15 kg	114 lb –126 lb	64.86 kg – 71.67 kg	143 lb – 158 lb
Large frame	55.34 kg – 62.14 kg	122 lb –137 lb	68.95 kg – 78.02 kg	152 lb – 172 lb

Height	1.60m	5 ft 3 in	1.80 m	5 ft 11 in
Small frame	50.35 kg – 53.98 kg	111 lb – 119 lb	63.96 kg – 68.49 kg	141 lb – 151 lb
Medium frame	53.07 kg – 58.51 kg	117 lb – 129 lb	66.68 kg – 73.94 kg	147 lb – 163 lb
Large frame	56.70 kg – 63.96 kg	125 lb – 141 lb	71.22 kg – 80.29 kg	157 lb – 177 lb

Height	1.63m	5 ft 4 in	1.83m	6 ft
Small frame	51.71 kg – 55.34 kg	114 lb – 122 lb	65.77 kg – 70.31 kg	145 lb – 155 lb
Medium frame	54.43 kg – 59.88 kg	120 lb – 132 lb	68.49 kg – 78.47 kg	151 lb – 173 lb
Large frame	58.06 kg – 65.77 kg	128 lb – 145 lb	75.30 kg – 84.82 kg	166 lb – 187 lb

Height	1.65m	5 ft 5 in	1.85m	6 ft 1 in
Small frame	53.07 kg – 57.15 kg	117 lb – 126 lb	67.59 kg – 72.58 kg	149 lb – 160 lb
Medium frame	55.79 kg – 61.69 kg	123 lb – 136 lb	70.31 kg – 78.47 kg	155 lb – 173 lb
Large frame	59.42 kg – 67.59 kg	131 lb – 149 lb	75.30 kg – 84.82 kg	166 lb – 187 lb

Height	1.68m	5 ft 6 in	1.88m	6 ft 2 in
Small frame	54.89 kg – 58.97 kg	121 lb – 130 lb	69.40 kg – 74.39 kg	153 lb – 164 lb
Medium frame	57.61 kg – 63.50 kg	127 lb – 140 lb	72.58 kg – 80.74 kg	160 lb – 178 lb
Large frame	61.24 kg – 69.85 kg	135 lb – 154 lb	77.57 kg – 87.09 kg	171 lb – 192 lb

Height	1.70m	5 ft 7 in	1.90m	6 ft 3 in
Small frame	56.70 kg – 60.78 kg	125 lb – 134 lb	71.21 kg – 76.21 kg	157 lb – 168 lb
Medium frame	59.42 kg – 65.77 kg	131 lb – 145 lb	74.84 kg – 83.01 kg	165 lb – 183 lb
Large frame	63.50 kg – 72.12 kg	140 lb – 159 lb	79.38 kg – 89.36 kg	175 lb – 197 lb

Height	1.72m	5 ft 8 in	1.92m	6 ft 4 in
Small frame	58.51 kg – 62.60 kg	129 lb – 138 lb	73.02 kg – 78.02 kg	161 lb – 172 lb
Medium frame	61.24 kg – 67.59 kg	135 lb – 149 lb	76.65 kg – 84.82 kg	169 lb – 187 lb
Large frame	65.32 kg – 73.94 kg	144 lb – 163 lb	81.19 kg – 91.17 kg	179 lb – 201 lb

Keeping a Record

Weigh yourself at the same time daily and record your weight in kg or lb on the charts provided below. Record your weight loss at

FORTNIGHT STARTING:

Day	1	2	3	4	5	6	7	Total
Week 1								
Week 2								
						Total weight loss		

FORTNIGHT STARTING:

Day	1	2	3	4	5	6	7	Total
Week 1								
Week 2								
						Total weight loss to date		

FORTNIGHT STARTING:

Day	1	2	3	4	5	6	7	Total
Week 1								
Week 2								
						Total weight loss to date		

the end of each week and the total weight loss at the end of the fortnight. You will feel more inclined to continue with the FBF Weight Loss Programme when you can chart your progress on paper and can see the weight literally falling away.

FORTNIGHT STARTING:

Day	1	2	3	4	5	6	7	Total
Week 1								
Week 2								
				Total weight loss to date				

FORTNIGHT STARTING:

Day	1	2	3	4	5	6	7	Total
Week 1								
Week 2								
				Total weight loss to date				

FORTNIGHT STARTING:

Day	1	2	3	4	5	6	7	Total
Week 1								
Week 2								
				Total weight loss to date				

frequently asked questions

Q I want to lose 3 kg (6¾ lb). How long should I stay on the programme?

A This depends on how quickly you lose the weight. The seven-day FBF Rapid Fat Loss Plan works as a complete nutritional unit, so remain on it for one to two weeks until you have reached your target weight. You can then stabilize your new weight with a fortnight on the FBF Stabilizer Plan of your choice.

Q What is meant by a week on the FBF Rapid Fat Loss Plan being a complete nutritional unit?

A The FBF Rapid Fat Loss Plan provides some of all the foods that the body needs over a period of seven days – geared to trigger rapid fat loss, of course. You can eat fresh negative calorie vegetables in unlimited quantities every day, certain fruits and fresh fruit juice on Days 1, 3, 4 and 7, dairy products on Day 4, low-GI carbohydrates and protein towards the end of the week, and so on. This is why you should remain on the diet for a whole 7- or 14-day period as described, before going on to the FBF Stabilizer Plan.

Q What if I want to lose only 1–1.75 kg (2–4 lb)?

A You should still complete the seven-day FBF Rapid Fat Loss Plan, even if you reach the target weight after a day or two. Then stabilize your weight loss by a fortnight on one of the FBF Stabilizer Plans because this acts as a guide to healthier everyday eating.

Q Supposing I become unwell while following the FBF Weight Loss Programme, what should I do?

A Just what you would normally do – try simple remedies for any symptoms that last for longer than a few hours, and consult your GP about any that persist. You should not be on the programme if you are pregnant or breastfeeding, and should check first with your doctor if you have any long-term medical condition.

Q Are there any side effects of the FBF Rapid Fat Loss Plan to watch out for?

A I am a great believer in mind over matter – many people are highly suggestible and providing them with a list of possible symptoms makes them very likely to experience them. However, the FBF Rapid Fat Loss Plan has a gently detoxing effect, which you can benefit from further by cutting out caffeine and drinking at least eight large (300 ml/½ pint) glasses of water a day. A very few people experience mild headaches, tiredness, irritability, a bad taste in the mouth and bad breath as toxins leave the system. Combat these with extra rest and relaxation, regular small snacks, skin brushing and a shoulder, neck and scalp massage.

Q I hate water. Can I drink unsweetened fruit juice in its place?

A Sorry, the answer is no. The FBF Rapid Fat Loss Plan is planned meticulously for maximum fat-burning effect, and you should eat and drink exactly what it recommends every day. Try tap water again (the flavour varies according to area), and experiment with the huge range of spring and mineral waters available. You can also drink your water hot, or chilled, on the rocks, with a thick slice of lemon or lime.

Q I've tried lots of diets since having my children but have never been able to lose more than 0.5–1 kg (1–2 lb). Why should I succeed on the FBF Weight Loss Programme?

A You haven't failed in the past – diets fail people, not the other way around. You have every chance of success on the FBF Rapid Fat Loss Plan, since it has been specially designed to burn surplus body fat that other diets have been unable to budge. It achieves this by boosting the body's fat-burning powers, targeting the possible underlying problem of a slow metabolism.

Q **I am getting married in three months' time and want to shed 19 kg (42 lb) quickly so I can buy a smaller wedding dress. Can't I just stay on the FBF Rapid Fat Loss Plan until I reach my goal?**

A I do empathize with your reasons for wanting to lose surplus fat quickly, but this is not the way to go about it. Most fit people could probably remain on the FBF Rapid Fat Loss Plan for considerably longer than a fortnight without developing nutritional deficiencies, but the plan's potent fat-busting action limits the intake of many foods normally enjoyed on a healthy diet. Also, two weeks of fat-burning alternating with two weeks of stabilizing has been shown, time and again, to shift fat fastest. You would be better following the plans as outlined, and building some regular fat-burning exercise (see page 119) into your daily schedule. Take daily supplements of multivitamins and minerals, plus 400 micrograms of chromium picolinate, for good measure.

Q **I don't eat any dairy products in any form, but get my calcium and magnesium from green leafy vegetables and a supplement (when I remember to take it). What can I do on day 4 of the FBF Rapid Fat Loss Plan where only bananas, skimmed milk (and the soup) are scheduled?**

A You sound in danger of developing a calcium deficiency, which can result in weak teeth and bones, and brittle bone disease (osteoporosis) in middle age. If you cannot take, or dislike, dairy products you should be substituting soya-derived milk, cheese, yogurts and so on. I suggest you make this alteration to your diet right away and use a reduced-fat soya milk in the diet to replace the cow's milk. Alternatives to soya milk are 'milks' made from barley, rice and wheat, but check their vitamin and mineral content. In your 20s you need around 1000 mg (1 g) of calcium daily, with half this amount of magnesium – more when you are older.

Q **I cannot stand vegetables apart from frozen peas. Can I still do the FBF Weight Loss Programme?**

A Vegetables are an essential element of the FBF Rapid Fat Loss Plan, and you cannot eat just peas all the time (or substitute fruit). And, unless you eat a great deal of fruit in the normal way, there is a chance that you may become deficient in the vitamins and minerals that vegetables supply. Try steaming mild-flavoured vegetables, such as swede or turnip, green beans, bamboo shoots or bean sprouts (see negative calorie foods list, page 27) or cooking them in a little clear chicken stock skimmed of fat (see page 37). Alternatively, purée them in a blender with a dash of low-sodium soy sauce or Worcestershire sauce. Farmhouse Dressing (see page 80) on very fresh, crisp lettuce or cress may tempt your taste buds, especially if you add masses of fresh herbs of your choice. However, an essential part of successful, maintained fat loss is choosing widely from foods you enjoy and if you truly cannot get to like vegetables, then the FBF Weight Loss Programme is not for you.

125

index

apples: apple and blueberry
    crumble 107
    traditional baked apple 103
apricots, Arabian 106
artichokes: artichoke, endive
    and green herb salad 76
    sautéed artichokes with Brazil
    nuts 99
avocado and prawns on rye 72

BMI (Body Mass Index) 17
BMR (basal metabolic rate) 7, 25
baked potato, spicy 40
baked vanilla custard 59
basal metabolic rate (BMR) 7, 25
Basic Stabilizer Plan see
    Stabilizer Plan, Basic
bean sprouts with soy and
    ginger 85
beans: green bean and egg
    salad 79
    warm bean salad with fresh
    herbs 78
beef, spiced, with apricots 56
blood sugar level 22
blueberry crumble, apple
    and 107
Body Mass Index (BMI) 17
boosting the fat-burning
    fires 112
braised vegetables with dill and
    mustard 37
breakfasts 34–35, 47, 48–49,
    64–69, 114
breathing, deep 118
brindleberry fruit 20, 26

carbohydrate foods 22, 23
carrot and celery juice 59
chicken: chicken and winter
    vegetables 89
    chicken antipasto 70
    harissa chicken with
    peppers 90
    home-made chicken stock 37
    Italian chicken with pan-fried
    vegetables 91
    lemon chicken stir-fry 57
chicory, orange and black olive
    salad 75
cholesterol 23
chromium 25, 26
citrus fruits 26
    fresh sardine salad and citrus
    mint tabbouleh 74
    minty citrus replete 101
cod's roe, smoked, with melba
    toast 73
coffee 113, 115
coleslaw: coleslaw with
    peanuts 50

slimmers' coleslaw 81
cottage cheese salsa on toast 72
courgettes: courgette stuffed
    mushrooms 84
    tomato and courgette bake 98
crab salad 82
creamy fish pie 54
custard, baked vanilla 59

daily allowance, Basic Stabilizer
    Plan 47
diabetes 25
dietary fats 24
dieting 6
diets, why others fail 110
dinners 34–35, 48–49, 64–69

eating, healthier 15
eating philosophy 45
eating plan 12
eggs: eggs Florentine 51
    green bean and egg salad 79
    truffle eggs 83
    wilted spinach with eggs and
    herb butter 83
energy, use of 7
Entertaining Stabilizer Plan 63,
    68–69
exercise, aerobic 113, 115, 118,
    119

fat-burner foods, making them
    work 114–115
Fat-burner Foods (FBF) Rapid Fat
    Loss Plan 34–35
    charting progress 31
    guidelines 33
    principles 32
    starting 30
    two weeks on/two weeks
    off 111
fat-burner foods solution 8–9
Fat-burner Foods Stabilizer Plans
    see Stabilizer Plans
Fat-burner Foods Weight Loss
    Programme 12
fat-burner steak Diane 86
fat-burning, accelerated 20
fat-burning protein foods 27
fat facts 6
fat loss 13, 17
fats, dietary 24
fish: creamy fish pie 54
    oily fish 24
    quick fish tartare 55
flageolet and mushroom
    savoury 100
food buying and cooking tips 45
foods
    availability of 15
    fat-burning protein 27

negative calorie 20, 21, 26, 27
    organic 32
    substitute 46, 62, 68
fresh sardine salad and citrus
    mint tabbouleh 74
fruit fanfare 102 see also citrus
    fruits

GI (glycaemic index) 22–23
GTF (glucose tolerance factor)
    chromium 25
gammon salad sandwich, toasted
    70
garlic steak with spring
    vegetables 87
genetic make-up 6–7
glucose 22, 26
glucose tolerance factor (GTF)
    chromium 25
glycaemic index (GI) 22–23
glycogen 26
goal setting 16
grape salad, melon and 38
'grazing' 44, 46, 62, 112, 114
green bean and egg salad 79
grill, mixed 89
grilled pears with oatmeal and
    raspberry cream 104

HCA (hydroxycitric acid) 20, 26
harissa chicken with peppers 90
health check 30
healthier eating 15, 32
herbs: herb-crusted lamb with
    spring greens 88
    herb omelette 85
honey yogurt, walnut and 102
hydroxycitric acid (HCA) 20, 26

insulin 20, 21, 22
iodine 25, 26
Italian chicken with pan-fried
    vegetables 91

Jerusalem artichoke soup 71

ketones/ketosis 14, 20
kidneys courtesan with Jamaican
    cabbage 56

lamb, herb-crusted, with spring
    greens 88
lemon chicken stir-fry 57
lentil soup, spicy 53
liver 56
lunches 34–35, 48–49, 64–69
Luxury Stabilizer Plan 62, 64–65
lychees with almond junket 105

mango smoothie 38
melon and grape salad 38

menu ideas 15
metabolic process 14, 20, 118
minty citrus replete 101
mixed grill 89
monkfish, sautéed, with green gem salad 94
mushrooms: courgette stuffed mushrooms 84
   flageolet and mushroom savoury 100

naturally occurring substances 20

ob-gene (obesity gene) 7
obesity 7–8, 17
oily fish 24
olive oil 24, 26
omelette, herb 85
oranges: chicory, orange and black olive salad 75
   orange pork 58
organic foods 15, 32
oriental risotto 41
'overweight', understanding 6
oxygen consumption 21

pasta with smoked salmon and asparagus 93
pears, grilled, with oatmeal and raspberry cream 104
persimmon cream 103
pineapple gratin, warm 104
pork, orange 58
positive indicators 31
prawns: avocado and prawns on rye 72
   prawns in brandy cream sauce 92
primavera stir-fry 38
protein, thermogenic effect of 20–21
protein foods, fat-burning 27

quick fish tartare 55
quick tomato soup 50

radish rocket salad 77
Rapid Fat Loss Plan see Fat-burner Foods Rapid Fat Loss Plan
redcurrant glass ceiling 106
rice salad, warm, with lemon, garlic and herbs 41
risotto, oriental 41

salad Niçoise 55
salmon: pasta with smoked salmon and asparagus 93
   salmon with lemon, parsley and tarragon 93

salt substitute 32
sardine, fresh, salad and citrus mint tabbouleh 74
satsuma and watercress salad 76
sausages, vegetarian, with tomato and herb mash 97
sautéed artichokes with Brazil nuts 99
sautéed monkfish with green gem salad 94
seafood: seafood and tomatoes on granary 52
   seafood vermicelli with tomato and mushroom sauce 95
slimmers' coleslaw 81
smoked cod's roe with melba toast 73
smoked trout and rainbow salad 80
soups: fat-burning soup 32, 36
   Jerusalem artichoke soup 71
   quick tomato soup 50
   spicy lentil soup 53
spiced beef with apricots 56
spiced turkey on a bed of potato 91
spicy baked potato 40
spicy foods 115
spicy lentil soup 53
spinach, wilted, with eggs and herb butter 83
spring onion salad, tomato and 73
Stabilizer Plan, Basic 46, 48–49
   breakfasts 47
   daily allowance 47
Stabilizer Plan, Entertaining 63, 68–69
Stabilizer Plan, Luxury 62, 64–65
Stabilizer Plan, Vegetarian 62, 66–67
Stabilizer plans, two weeks on/two weeks off 111
stabilizer principles 44
steak: fat-burner steak Diane 86
   garlic steak with spring vegetables 87
steamed vegetables with guacamole topping 99
stir-fry, primavera 39
strawberries with crême fraîche and Grand Marnier 101
stuffed tomatoes 81

tea 113, 115
thyroid gland 25
toasted gammon salad sandwich 70
tomatoes: quick tomato soup 50
   seafood and tomatoes on

granary 52
   stuffed tomatoes 81
   tomato and courgette bake 98
   tomato and spring onion salad 73
   viva tomatoes on toast 75
traditional baked apple 103
trout, smoked, and rainbow salad 80
truffle eggs 83
turkey, spiced, on a bed of potato 91

variations 46, 62, 68
veal schnitzel with spinach and Brazil nuts 87
vegetables 125
   braised vegetables with dill and mustard 37
   steamed vegetables with guacamole topping 99
vegetarian sausages with tomato and herb mash 97
Vegetarian Stabilizer Plan 62, 66–67
viva tomatoes on toast 75

walnut and honey yogurt 102
warm bean salad with fresh herbs 78
warm pineapple gratin 104
warm rice salad with lemon, garlic and herbs 41
water, drinking 33, 114
watercress salad, satsuma and 76
weighing daily 31
Weight Loss Programme, Fat-Burner Foods 12
weight reduction, fast 13
weight training 118
whiting stoker with green beans and cayenne potato 96
wilted spinach with eggs and herb butter 83

acknowledgements

Octopus Publishing Group Limited/David Jordan front cover right, front cover centre, front cover centre right, 6 bottom right (repeated throughout), 6 bottom left (repeated throughout), 6 bottom centre left (repeated throughout), 6 bottom centre right (repeated throughout), 7 bottom right (repeated throughout), 7 bottom left (repeated throughout), 7 bottom centre (repeated throughout), 7 bottom centre left (repeated throughout), 8 bottom right (repeated throughout), 8 bottom left (repeated throughout), 8 bottom centre (repeated throughout), 8 bottom centre left (repeated throughout), 8 bottom centre right (repeated throughout), 9 bottom left (repeated throughout), 9 bottom centre (repeated throughout), 9 bottom centre left (repeated throughout), 9 bottom centre right (repeated throughout), 29 bottom right, 36, 39, 53, 57, 58, 71, 74, 78, 82, 84, 90, 92, 93, 95, 97, 98, 104, 107/Ian Wallace front cover centre left (repeated throughout), 6 bottom centre (repeated throughout)/Jeremy Hopley front cover left (repeated throughout), 7 bottom centre right (repeated throughout), 9 bottom right (repeated throughout)

Commissioning Editor: Nicky Hill
Project Editors: Sarah Ford and
   Jo Lethaby
Index: Alan Thatcher

Executive Art Editor: Leigh Jones
Designer: Bill Mason

Photographer: Dave Jordan
Food Stylist: Oona van den Berg
Stylist: Clare Hunt

Production Controller: Viv Cracknell